I0468208

A turbulent career

Five stories, starting with Nortel

By

Victor Bellini

Five stories of business triumphs & failures including:

Nortel - *A large multinational*
IPS - *A high-tech start-up*
Spar Aerospace - *A medium-sized corporation*
Sovcanstar - *An international Joint Venture*
NSI - *A small public company*

Copyright © 2016 by Vittorio Bellini

Second Edition

ISBN-13: 978-1523867189
ISBN-10: 1523867183

Also by Vittorio (Victor) Bellini

Adventures in Multinational Business
- The Libyan Affair
- The Casablanca Connection
-The Russian Oligarch
- The Mexican Seduction
- The Chinese Manuscript

Other novels
- A girl named Gioia
- La mano del destino (in Italian)
- The Union
- Inspired in Venice
- Of Human Emotions
- Broken Dreams
- Once Upon a Time

Short stories:
- One-night Stands
-Revolutionary times

Biographies:
- Amen!
- A turbulent career
- Delusional Paranoia

Available in digital and paperback formats
from most online bookstores

For information: leopardpress@outlook.com

Foreword

This story is truthful to a fault and focuses on my business experience in five different high-tech companies, starting with the economic hay-days of the seventies, the advent of digital technologies of the eighties, the quantum leaps of the internet era of the nineties, and the eventual dotcom collapse in the first few years of the new millennium.

It all started at Northern Electric (Nortel), Montreal, in 1967 and continued with postings in Toronto, London, Rome, Algiers, Miami and back to Montreal, with special missions in Russia and China, along with further business dealings in Mexico City, Caracas, Buenos Aires and Los Angeles. The five stories are written in chronological order, reflecting my career changes.

The events chronicled in this book show the dangers of being rewarded with early success in business, as overconfidence leads to arrogance which, in turn, leads to disrespect for others and eventual downfall. Learning from the experience of others can help avoid costly mistakes.

PART ONE

Life at Nortel 1967-1990

***

Chapter One

Northern Electric

I arrived in Montreal on a very cold February 6, 1967, at the age of twenty-five, with $500 in cash and a suitcase of clothes. Two days later I lost my wallet and all the cash (sic!), but also found a temporary $2/hr job as technician in the repair shop of a Radio-TV sales outlet. Four months thereafter, on June 6, I was hired by Northern Electric (later known as Nortel Networks) as an electronic technician. At the time NE was a $500 million wholly owned subsidiary of Bell Canada, with some 15,000 employees.

I was happy to be part of what was considered a major corporation and see my career move in the direction I always wanted it to move. My new job gave me plenty of satisfaction as I soon proved to be overqualified for what I was doing. However, less than a month after starting, salary negotiations between union and company broke down. I therefore found myself on strike, with debt and no income.

The strike lasted six weeks, during which time I became friends with Suria, an immigrant of Indian origins from Tanzania, who worked in the same department. Suria had immigrated a year earlier and took evening classes in engineering, which was what I also wanted to do to finish what I started in England. At the end of the strike I returned to work with renewed enthusiasm and a slightly higher paycheck at $2.75/hr. I soon gained popularity in the department and made friends quickly.

A couple of months later, in the late summer of 1967, I was able to trade in a rusty Beetle I had bought soon after my arrival in Montreal for a newer car, a three-year old Corvair with the engine in the back. It was the GM challenge to the VW Beetle, but turned out to be a nightmare of minor breakdowns.

In the meantime I was being 'noticed' at work for my performance, to the point that some of my colleagues asked me to slow down, as I was upsetting some of the existing productivity standards they were being held to. We were about twenty technicians at various levels in the department. We diagnosed and repaired various types of electronic test instruments used by telephone companies. Each of those instruments had been

7

benchmarked in terms of repair time for productivity purposes. I was approached by one of my colleagues who told me in a friendly but firm tone of voice something like this:

"You are not doing anyone any favor by working the way you do. Just relax and take it easy."

"Why, what's the problem?" I asked.

"The problem is that if you keep that up they will demand higher productivity from the rest of us."

"I am sorry," I replied, "I am only doing what I am paid to do. I can't just sit on my ass and do nothing half the time!"

"Well, I don't know how you do it, but just reading the procedures takes a lot of time," he said.

"Why do you need to read the procedures?" I asked.

"That's what we are told to do. How can you test and diagnose anything if you don't follow the steps listed in the manual?"

"Well, I am sorry, but I don't need to read the manual. I know what to look for and what to do."

"Okay then, maybe you should not be in this department. Anyway, you should respect others and slow down. Walk around, talk to people, go to the coffee machine more often."

"I understand," I said. "I'll do my best."

He was not a happy camper, that's for sure. As it turned out, I did not have to change my work habits at all, because I was quickly upgraded to the top grade and still performed above standards. In October that same year, barely four months after I started, I was interviewed for a desk-bound engineering job and was then re-assigned to the equipment engineering offices located in downtown Montreal. I was thrilled. Wow! I was no longer unionized and my salary took a leap forward. I was to wear suit and tie in an office building right at the crossroads of Ste. Catherine & Stanley, the very heart of downtown Montreal!

That was the first indication of the kind of company NE was. In less than four months they recognized the worth of an employee and rewarded him without hesitation. There was no red tape, no forms to fill, no waiting period, nothing of the sort. They noticed 'value' and they secured it. I was impressed.

The advantages of working downtown were enormous, for I was able to just walk to the university campus on Guy Street after work for my evening classes. As well, the company policy was to encourage further education for all employees and pay for all evening courses related to their job. Consequently, I was reimbursed for every penny I spent on student fees and textbooks for all my courses. What started as a job to help me through college turned out to be, in a sense, a university in its own right, for NEC was much more than a company in those days; it was an institution, an alma mater and almost a family to me.

All my friends in those early days were office colleagues, a mix of married and single men and women with whom I shared many lunch hours and after-work drinks. They were happy people, with secure jobs and financially stable. In that carefree environment, I also met my future wife, at which time my plan for a return to Italy was forever shelved.

Engineering studies

As an evening student in electrical engineering at Sir George Williams University (later Concordia) I did well for a couple of years till I got married and became a father in 1970. The thrill of fatherhood, coupled with the extra time and attention it required, made it difficult to handle the work load. As a result, I dropped out of college for a while and focused entirely on family needs and on my career at NE. I resumed my studies in 1971, following special permission from the Dean of Engineering, and completed the third academic year for a B.Eng. in 1972. For the final year, however, evening classes were not available.

At that point, I would have had to attend full time to graduate, something I could not afford to do. However, the Ordre des Ingenieurs du Quebec, or OIQ, (the provincial association of professional engineers) made it possible for 'mature' engineering candidates like me to write the final exams on five subjects without attending university. Having been working in an engineering capacity at Nortel for four years already, and having been recommended by two licensed engineers, in addition to my manager, I was deemed to have met all of the OIQ prerequisites and was therefore allowed to write the final year exams for a B.Sc. in electrical engineering.

To prepare for the exams, I was given a list of assigned textbooks and access to past exam papers. My department manager was so helpful that he gave me permission to seek help from graduate engineers in the department. He also allowed me to use of a small office cubicle and time off normal duties for as long as necessary to prepare for my exams. I could not have asked for better treatment. Northern proved once again to be a unique employee-friendly company, the likes of which I have never seen again anywhere. It's been my de-facto alma mater.

The OIQ authorization documents for my final exams were completed during a period of major organizational changes at NE, changes that eventually resulted in my transfer to Toronto in July 1973, as will be seen in more details in the next chapter. They OIQ documents were therefore transferred to the Professional Engineers of Ontario in Toronto. They then set the date and supervised the exams at their offices over five consecutive days. As I passed them all, including an additional one on Professional Ethics, I was given a seal and licensed to practice without further ado as a Professional Engineer.

It was the end of a ten-year-long quest that started in 1964, when I left Tripoli for London. I received an immediate upgrade to 'full engineer' status at NE, thereby bypassing the two-year in-training period normally expected of new graduates.

***

Chapter Two

The visionaries of the seventies

Starting in 1971 major organizational changes were being made under the leadership of a new CEO, John Lobb. He evolved the company from a complacent 'captive-market' laggard to a dynamic no-nonsense company, aggressive enough to more than quadruple its net profit in the first two years of his leadership. He transformed the company in many ways and established a presence in the USA with a plant in Michigan. He also gave the company independence from its previous association with Western Electric. At the time Northern operated under technology license for telecom switching products from its American counterpart and was therefore limited in its proprietary offerings.

Western Electric was the largest manufactures of telecom equipment at the time and was part of an American tri-corporate behemoth that included Western Electric, Bell Labs and AT&T. It was a business model that appealed to Lobb so much that he eventually copied it by forming BNR (Bell-Northern Research labs), owned 50-50 by Bell Canada and Northern Electric.

I still remember a departmental meeting we had when the creation of BNR was announced after the official split from Western Electric. Our manager briefed us on the significance of that transformation. He said in part (paraphrased):

"You know, this is a game changer for this company. It means that we will have to create our own technology because we can no longer use design blueprints from Western. In other words, our limited operations in R&D will have to be boosted massively to enable us to design our own equipment. It's going to be a task of enormous proportions. So ... fasten your seat belts and be prepared for anything."

"May I ask a question?" said Dieter, a German engineer and a close friend of mine.

"Sure, go ahead."

"Will we have a chance to move to BNR if we choose to do so? I do have experience from my days at Siemens and I would love to get back into R&D activities."

"I suppose that you can apply if that's what you want. But don't hold your breath. A lot of organizational changes have yet to be implemented and, you know, there is also an important financing question."

"That was my question," said another engineer. "If we are to set up the equivalent of Bell Labs in Canada, where will the money come from?"

"Quite frankly," he replied with a chuckle, "I don't know. My guess is that Bell Canada will foot the bill initially. Later, who knows, they will probably float some shares or go for an IPO. Whatever Mr. Lobb wants to do, he didn't tell me! All I can tell you is that BNR will have to grow very fast in future."

We all laughed. Obviously the steps required for the transformation of a second-tier manufacturing company into an independent technology leader were being held close to the chest by the top brass. Once again I was impressed by the vision and the determination shown by top management, given the financial risk inherent in their plan.

Later that year, 1973, Northern went public with an IPO and floated 10% of Bell Canada's shares, thereby reducing it from 100% to 90%. At that point we all knew that we were part of a tri-corporate organization, much like our neighbors to the south. Northern Electric was to Bell Canada what Western Electric was to AT&T; and BNR was to Northern what Bell Labs was to Western. *Les jeux sont faits!*

The Canadian version of the American tri-corporate organization was thus complete and ready to compete head to head with their America counterparts. As a result, Northern quickly became Western Electric's foe, as they challenged each other on the development and deployment of a new family of telecom equipment.

The R&D factor

In parallel with Lobb's appointment as CEO of Northern, in 1971 Don Chisholm was appointed President of the Research Labs (later renamed as BNR) with a very specific mission. He was tasked with growing it fast by staffing it with scientists and engineers from anywhere in the world. They could not have asked a better man for the job. Don managed the company like a university campus, recruiting qualified people – usually engineers degreed with bachelors, or masters or doctorates - wherever he could find them, and inspiring them to work as a unified team with one and only one purpose -- go digital for everything needed in a telecom network.

Along with the creation of BNR, John Lobb made it possible to change the corporate name of the company from the old and ill-representative 'Northern Electric', to the new and more reflective of what the company did 'Northern Telecom', or NT. It was a master stroke of sorts, as it gave the company a new identity partially divorced from the Bell Canada, and gave it the possibility of being traded on its own right.

Moving from an analog technology to a digital one was a tall order, of course. The digitization of speech, for instance, was still in its infancy and had yet to be conclusively proven in terms of quality, reliability and economics. Breaking up analogical sound waves into streams of binary bits required fast processing and cost-effective memory banks not yet available in those days. All R&D labs of major telecom equipment manufacturers were trying to get it done.

Another important part of going digital was the need to create a parallel team of designers dedicated to software programming. The two teams, hardware and software, were then required to work together on any new product, something that differed considerably from designing computers, which were mostly limited to executing commands on a screen without triggering servomechanisms. Given all of those unknowns, the overall digitization mandate was a colossal management gamble that could have bankrupted the company very quickly. But it worked and it made the company a world leader in digital telecom networks.

I saw the first demonstration of a digital voice recording in Bramalea in 1974, given in theatrical form by a BNR engineer. It was still rudimentary, still crude on dynamic range and frequency response, but it proved that it was possible. Not long thereafter the methodology was defined and normalized at an international conference in Geneva. Several companies had contributed to its standardization and it soon became adopted in all kinds of different applications.

In addition to digitizing voice, the other major hurdle was to make it possible to switch voice channels digitally, without huge mechanical banks of switches. I remember visiting a public switching exchange in Toronto serving 400,000 subscribers in 1975. It consisted of several floors of huge barn-like rooms filled with rows and rows of noisy mechanical switches, constantly clicking away to cross connect subscribers to telephone calls to and from anywhere.

At that time the system used was the so-called Cross-Bar, which replaced older and bulkier Step-by-Step system. They required a lot of maintenance and took a lot of electric power and floor space. It was estimated that if switching could be digitized, the gain in power, floor space and maintenance costs would be slashed by more than an order of magnitude. In other words, the same exchange serving

400,000 subscribers could be contained on a silent single floor, rather than seven noisy ones. It was therefore a no-brainer to go all out on its development.

Transfer to Toronto

As part of these revolutionary changes, (coupled with separatist activities in the Province of Quebec), NT decided to consolidate its engineering expertise in Ontario and built a large plant in Bramalea, a Toronto suburb. It was designed to house both a branch-lab for BNR engineers and manufacturing facilities for switching technologies. Consequently, in the summer of 1973 my department of system engineers, including myself, was transferred to Toronto. We were allowed substantial benefits to help resettle, including a lump sum of money for moving costs and for an interest-free five-year loan to help with the difference in real estate prices between Montreal and Toronto.

This turn of events coincided with the birth of my second son, Marc, and allowed me to buy my first home, a small three-bedroom townhouse in Meadowvale, Mississauga, where we settled down as a family of four. A few months later, as mentioned earlier, I wrote my final engineering exams in Toronto, and graduated in May 1974. My position at Nortel was then reclassified along with a substantial salary increase.

The reclassification opened the doors to a more rewarding career path. As engineers we were graded within the management ranks, thereby leading to the top. New graduates started at grade seven, while senior engineers were grade eleven, at which point a select few were tested to identify management material. The ones so identified were then sent on a series of courses to be groomed for management positions, starting at grade 12 as first level section managers. I was initially classified at grade nine, but a year later I was upgraded to the top.

Not long thereafter I was enrolled in a series of most enlightening and rewarding management courses. They were eye-openers, for they taught me valuable techniques in overall planning, timing, controlling, budgeting and forecasting. They were techniques that could be applied equally well in private life and changed forever the way I tackled any problem, whether at work or at home. To these days, I always wonder whether there is a more effective way of doing whatever it is that I do. In those days, every engineering department had a training budget for its employees. Part of the training was to keep technical staff current on technology trends and part was to identify talented employees for a future in management.

That same year, in late 1975, one important event changed forever my career at NT. Six senior engineers, including myself, from different departments had been selected for two days and two nights of some sort of training session held in a hotel away from home. We were not told the real purpose for the session, so we did not know what to expect. We spent the first evening socializing and were then asked to show up the following morning at a small conference room for a brainstorming session on productivity. The idea was to compare notes on the way we operated in our respective departments.

I remember sitting in that conference room, all six of us, at nine o'clock sharp, notebook in hand, ready to take notes and waiting for the session leader. He was late, very late. Some twenty minutes later I walked to the whiteboard and addressed my colleagues. I told them that it being a brainstorming session on productivity, we knew what was expected of us and that we should get going without further ado. They agreed after some hesitation and we started discussing the way we did things in our respective departments. The session leader showed up only much later and announced with a smile that he was deliberately absent to see if anyone of us would take the lead. It was meant to be a test on initiative and leadership.

The next morning we were subjected to another test. Each one of us was given a separate room with a desk, pencil, notepad and an in-basket full of notes, memos and reports. We were supposed to be the CEO of a large company, due to fly overseas on a one-week business trip. We only had two hours to go through the in-basket and leave appropriate instructions on whatever needed to be done. The exercise was intended to test our decision-making abilities and see how fast we were able to understand the issues and provide appropriate instructions on all action items.

I don't know how well I did because we were not given any feedback on that particular test, but I do know that two of us were quickly promoted to management in different departments, while the other four remained in engineering. That was the beginning of a fast moving management career for me, something that gave me confidence beyond all expectations.

*

The Walter Light years
In 1974 Walter Light was appointed CEO and continued forcefully along the path of John Lobb, with the same aggressive style

and ambitious program. In the meantime major strides forward were being made at BNR. They managed to switch digitally voice channels and thereby produce an alternative to large and expensive banks of mechanical switches. The new technology was seen as revolutionary in the mid seventies and the future of telephony was clearly seen as belonging to fully digital switching systems.

Several competing companies in North America, Western Europe and Japan worked feverishly to be the first off the mark. Northern chose to invest all it had on it and was successful in bringing to market a small version of the very first fully digital switching system. It was a PBX (Private Business Exchanges), known as SL-1. It was installed as a field trial system at a Bell Canada site in 1975. The system proved to be a success story. As a flamboyant risk taker, Walter did not hesitate in redefining and restructuring the company to position it for global markets.

What Don Chisholm did for BNR, Walter Light did for Northern. Both of them were the innovators par excellence, the visionaries that made a huge difference to the future of the company. Walter guided it through a decisive no-nonsense expansion program designed to use our technology as leverage in the highly competitive international arena. Given the relatively small size of the company in those days and considering the initial investment needed to break into virgin territory around the world, it must have been a very risky decision to make.

In 1976 the newly reinvented Northern Telecom went international and started to open offices around the world that eventually led to the creation of wholly owned subsidiaries. Thus NT-Canada, NT-USA, NT-Europe, NT-Asia and also NT-CALA were born, all of them reporting to the holding company NT Limited, headquartered in Toronto. A few short years later the corporation was well poised for major gains in the USA and opened its largest manufacturing facilities in Raleigh, NC, while international markets were being probed with sales offices in Zurich, London, Sydney, Tokyo and Miami for CALA.

By 1978, the very first digital Public Exchange known as DMS (Digital Multiplex System) was field trialed at another Bell Canada site with enormous success. Soon thereafter several multinational companies came up with competing systems, but NT retained a substantial edge in terms of reliability and performance. It became obvious at that point that the company had a trump card up its sleeve and was ready to compete anywhere.

At that time, however, NT was barely visible outside of Canada, as most of its business was with its parent company and other Canadian telecom operators. The offices opened around the world were still being staffed and not yet fully operational. But, despite the drawbacks, the confidence level was very high, and a sense of complacency took root in everybody's mind. It was just the beginning of what would eventually become a major international success story and would lead to what became known as Vision-2000.

It was a bold declaration made in 1987 to hundreds of Forbe's-500 CEOs and their consorts held 'captive' on a cruise ship. The objective was for NT to be - by year 2000 - the Numero Uno of telecom equipment manufacturers in the world, with some $30 billion in revenue.

***

Chapter Three

CALRS

In 1976 Bell Canada, smarting from the early success with digital applications, decided to undertake an ambitious project aimed at automating their Repair Service Centers using minicomputers. They produced a wish list of system requirements and mandated BNR to assess its technical feasibility. Following an initial conceptual design, Bell and NT agreed to do a joint market study to determine its commercial viability, following which they decided to proceed with the development of a sophisticated minicomputer system known as CALRS (Centralized Automated Loop Reporting System).

At that point in time Repair Service Centers were organized in several distinct sections. Answer operators, mostly women, took 611 calls from subscribers having problems with their telephone line and recorded the problem on what was known as a 'trouble ticket'. The ticket was then passed on by conveyor belt to a group of analysts who looked for a 'history' file for that particular telephone line. The history and the trouble tickets were then moved to the first available tester, or expert technician. He would then undertake a series of tests on the line to identify the problem. Once the problem was identified it went onto a team of schedulers to assign a time slot for the repair.

That system was clearly time-consuming, as it took several minutes to diagnose a problem. It therefore begged to be automated, but it was not an easy task, as it implied building a sophisticated data base and an automated system to do all physical tests on the line without human intervention. It was possible in theory, but it had never been attempted before.

Four teams were assigned to work on the project. NT was the prime mover with overall control, while Bell was the user authority. BNR was responsible for the bulk of the computer hardware and software design while a fourth party, Northeast Electronics (NE), based in Concord, New Hampshire, was responsible for the hardware needed to do automated line testing. NE was a wholly owned subsidiary of Nortel at the time.

I was appointed Project Manager and was assigned two senior engineers to help me coordinate all scheduling and budgeting activities related to the project, including monitoring BNR and NE technical progress and budget expenses.

The system was conceived on using minicomputers and hard drives. It consisted of two parts. The first was a data base to store subscriber information, (name, address, type of service, equipment, history of trouble reports and notes) of all subscribers served by a particular exchange. The other part was the actual line testing, normally done manually by trained technicians. They tested for loop continuity, resistance, inductance, capacitance, ringer presence, voltage and leakage to ground.

CALRS was expected to automate both parts, thereby reducing the overall time needed to process a trouble report from several minutes to just a few seconds. The net result was expected to be a substantial service improvement and a significant reduction in the number of operators and testers employed in each service center.

The initial business plan assumed a price of two-million dollar for a system serving up to 500,000 subscribers, with a payback time of approximately two years. The calculation was based on time studies done at two exchanges in Ottawa and in Las Vegas. The business case looked good on paper and was enthusiastically supported by both Bell and NT, but BNR reserved judgment, noting that we were breaking new grounds on the use of minicomputers that were still evolving and were not yet powerful enough for the task.

As the Project Manager for NT, I was a member of the Steering Committee and chaired weekly Working Committee meetings. Given the complexity of the project, technical problems were a daily occurrence, whether from the hardware or the software side. The use of minicomputers and mass media storage devices for telephony applications had never been tackled before and proved to be full of bad surprises. After a lot of initial work it was determined that one mini (PDP-11 from DEC) could not handle the load. But the use of two minis would upset the economics of the project and would impose a new design approach. Reliability issues required full system redundancy, meaning that each system had to have an identical one in stand-by mode. Four minis were therefore needed, rather than two.

After a lot of deliberations it was decided to try a new design approach to minimize costs. Three minis would be connected via a special high-speed 'bus' in a ring configuration. That way it was possible to have full redundancy with three minis rather than four. DEC (Digital Equipment Corporation) was then commissioned to develop such special high-speed link, or bus, thereby making them another design partner to contend with.

The Business Plan had to be revised at that point. The new numbers did not support the commercial viability of the project, which risked being cancelled. However, because a lot of development money had already been spent, Bell decided to bite the bullet and commit to purchasing enough systems at a higher price to make it worthwhile for NT. The project was therefore restarted on a higher budget and a new schedule.

In those days, however, there was a lot of guesswork involved estimating the time required to write software program for minicomputer systems. It was not an exact science. Scheduling completion dates was therefore a hit and miss exercise. As well, software quality issues required frequent rework and made it difficult to meet important milestones. We realized after a few setbacks that the situation could not be sustained and that new ways of estimating and controlling software development were needed.

At an international conference on software development in New York - attended by Mehmet Ficici, the QA engineer on my team - some panelists argued very convincingly that software development was in fact more of an art than a science, whose quality could only be assessed after a period of operation in real time. There was a lot of truth in it, but it was not an acceptable modus operandi for competing businesses.

I remember a conversation I had with Mehmet when he returned from that conference.

"Those guys think they are artists not engineers," he said with a smile. "They claim that it's impossible to estimate how long it takes to develop a fully reliable software module. So, I told them that we, at NT, are not running an art gallery!"

I laughed. "So, what did they say to that?"

"They laughed at first, but then I discussed the problem separately with some of them and we agreed that we could do a better job at controlling quality if we break down the software modules into much smaller units, with clearly defined inputs and outputs. That way we can follow the progress more closely and much more effectively, and catch smaller problems before they become big problems."

Eventually the design team agreed to proceed that way. It did not prove to be the panacea to all our software problems, but it did show growing improvements, with less rework and more reliability. It was the beginning of major changes in software development that made it possible to estimate more accurately time and cost requirements.

On the hardware development side, things were more predictable, but were still riddled with delays and overruns, primarily due to the automated line testing which was planned to take no more than 20 seconds, but required well over 40 seconds in its initial version.

Testing time was crucial to make the system cost-effective and competitive. Northeast Electronics specialized in testing instruments and was in charge of developing that part of CALRS, but its engineers were somewhat disorganized and needed to be closely watched, which made me fly to Concord more frequently than I wanted to. They argued that it was impossible to meet the 20 seconds target, but after several attempts, they delivered. The testing time did come down to 16 seconds or better - a substantial improvement from the several minutes required by manual means - and was therefore accepted as 'mission accomplished'.

The project was completed in its initial version in late 1978, three years after the initial idea. Two successful field trials took place in Ottawa and in Las Vegas, each serving some 500,000 subscribers. In 1979, despite a strong union opposition who worried about the loss of jobs, the project was approved for implementation at all repair service sites within Bell Canada. It was then decided to market the system to all service providers, nationally and internationally.

As a result, in 1979 I was appointed marketing manager, in charge of promoting CALRS sales globally. My new appointment gave me another management upgrade, along with a staff of two engineers and a yearly budget that included a substantial amount for training. I took advantage of that opportunity and signed up for more management courses, including one on negotiating skills. I thus discovered a side of myself I did not know I had. I was a strategist, very good at preparing and delivering persuasive slide presentations on the benefits and economics of CALRS, tailored to the needs of specific customers. It was a skill that was soon noticed by upper management. Before long, CALRS landed on the radar screen of sales staff in Zurich, where the HQ of NT-Europe was located.

In mid-1980 I was contacted by the NT salesman in charge of Germany and Austria. He informed me that there was keen interest in CALRS from the Austrian PTT (PostTelephone&Telegraph), and that I was invited to make a presentation in Vienna to the PTT authorities. I studied the Austrian telephone network and prepared a specific application plan on a slide presentation.

I flew to Vienna via Paris and suffered my first setback. The flight arrived very late in Paris and made me miss the connection to Vienna. After a lot of aggravation I took a flight to Munich with connection to Vienna, where I arrived very late in the evening, but without my luggage, which got lost somewhere.

Fortunately I had my briefcase and slides with me and was therefore able to be on time at the meeting, but in jeans and an open shirt. I apologized profusely for looking the way I did to the well-dressed high-ranking audience, but they laughed it off and assured me that they understood and did not mind. Somehow I warmed up to the audience and gave them a compelling presentation on CALRS, along with a suggested plan for the entire Austrian network. Before closing, I remember a comment made by the Director General of the PTT when I stressed the economic benefits.

"As you can see," I concluded with some swagger, *"the five systems we recommend for your national network would significantly reduce the space requirements and the number of operators,, with equivalent gains in cost and productivity."*
The DG of the PTT seemed amused at my statement and told me in excellent English.

"Quite honestly, Mr. Bellini, in Austria we do not see economics the way you do in North America. We have no interest in reducing our staff. We are only interested in improving and expanding our services."

That comment made me think long and hard about the difference in the set of social values between North America and Europe. Our goal was to save money and increase profitability, while theirs was to provide better services for the same budget.

I returned to my hotel after the meeting and found my luggage in my room. In the evening I had dinner with Hugh Hamilton, the President of NT-Europe. He congratulated me and told me the presentation was well received, but needed to be followed up with a detailed study to determine their exact needs. I took that opportunity to ask him a question

"What do you think of the DG comment on staff reduction and profitability?" I asked.

"Well, that's a lesson for you," he replied with a fatherly attitude. "Most countries in Europe, especially Austria, sit on the left of the political spectrum and are therefore somewhat socialistic. In the public sector, such as the PTT and many other state-run institutions, they care more about the well being of people than they do about the bottom

line. Keep that in mind when you present CALRS to other PTTs in Europe. Place the emphasis on quality, productivity and service improvements, not on how many operators they can fire!"

He then told me that France, Belgium and the UK were also interested and that I should make plans to meet with them too. He also asked me how many languages I spoke and other personal and family questions. At the end, as we returned to the hotel, he asked me if I would be interested in eventually moving to the Maidenhead offices in England. I told him enthusiastically that I would be more than just interested.

For nearly a year following that first meeting, I travelled back and forth to Vienna, Paris, Zurich, Brussels, Bonn and London to introduce and develop CALRS plans for those markets. I also spent an entire summer month in Paris (I took the entire family with me) to lead a joint team of engineers from NT and the French PTT to study the possibility of using CALRS for their network. True to their nature, however, we quickly found out that the French were more interested in learning about our design than they were in purchasing our systems. Be it as it may, NT was paid a million French francs for that study.

In the meantime my family needs kept on growing and space requirements for my three boys increased. I purchased a much larger house, newly built in a Bramalea subdivision, and moved there in June 1980, which coincided with my first trip to Vienna.

A year later, in early 1981, I was offered an expatriate management position in the UK, which implied moving the whole family to England. The financial benefits of the position, which included a significant management upgrade, were too good to refuse and I therefore accepted after discussing the pros and cons with my wife and children. A few months later, in June 1981, we moved and settled down in Maidenhead, Berkshire, near London.

***

Chapter Four

The eighties

Life in England proved to be very different for my family, but for me it was like a trip down memory lane. The city of London evoked in me youthful times of my student days. They were times of fun and games, of discovery and self-awareness; they were times of multiple romances and of dealing with cultural differences that deepened my understanding of human emotions. But in spite of all the pleasant memories, my being there again after fourteen years of absence did not awaken feelings of nostalgia or regrets of any kind. I looked at it as a different era, appropriate to a different and much younger person.

As a student in those days I was an idealist. I wanted to change the world and was quick to criticize democratic institutions and life styles, without actually knowing enough about democracy. I was a typical youth, a bit of an intellectual, full of dreams and somewhat naive. Fourteen years later, having grown beyond that stage and having family responsibilities, I looked back at those years with a dismissive smile. I had no desire, none at all, to be that young again. I was living through a fourth phase of my life, following my sad childhood, my turbulent youth, my family life and, finally, my career.

After living in a Maidenhead hotel for a couple of weeks, we rented a furnished house in Wargrave, a small town near Maidenhead; enrolled the boys in private schools; purchased some additional household items, a TV set and a Stereo system, and moved in. We all looked happy and enthusiastic, but deep inside I had some concerns. I was worried about my wife and three young boys. I was forewarned that adjusting to a new lifestyle and new friends was not going to be easy for the family, but they took it in stride, as an adventure, and seemed happy and excited about their new home and their different life.

The Maidenhead office was in charge of the Middle East and Africa (ME&A), with Brian Baynes as Managing Director. I was in charge of all of Africa, both anglophone and francophone, and was simply told to develop that market for all NT product lines, including transmission equipment, of which I new very little. I started working without knowing where to start and what exactly I was expected to do.

I had no idea of how to go about breaking into a new and foreign marketplace.

Brian was a no-nonsense kind of man in his mid-forties, of Welsh origins, well groomed, driven and self-assured. He spoke with confidence and authority as I sat in front of him in his extra-large office and listened carefully to what he had to say.

"Our mission is to grow the market as fast as we can," he said. "We need to make this organization profitable in the next couple of years. At present we are not, because our sales volume is insufficient to generate enough cash to cover our costs, but I am confident that the potential is there."

"May I ask you a question?" I said.

"Sure, shoot."

"What's the break-even point? I mean what sales volume do we need to achieve to break even?"

"Well, that's a good question. The answer depends on many things. Right now we are in market penetration mode and we must focus on sales rather than profit. Our prices are therefore low and our gross margin is also low. That's part of the problem. The other part of the problem is that we are not yet well known around the world. Canada is not viewed as a high-tech country, not yet anyway, so we have to overcome that notion."

"Okay, I see what you mean." I said thoughtfully. *"In other words, we have to sell the country first, the company next and then the product."*

"That's exactly right."

"I understand, but what do we have in the budget for the current fiscal year? I mean, what are the top and bottom line targets we are expected to meet?"

He looked at me for a few seconds with curiosity, as if he did not expect that kind of question. He then smiled and leaned forward on his desk.

"I can see that you have been well trained in financial stuff," he said. *"I like that, but you should not worry about budget commitments at this stage. We review our budget numbers quarterly and make adjustments, if necessary, based on the latest forecast. Our fiscal year ends in December, in line with Corporate, so we only have four useful months left this year. The financial targets will surely be met with a couple of projects we already have in the pipeline."*

"I suppose that Africa is not yet on your radar screen," I noted with a smile.

"No, it is not. I have zero revenue in the budget for this year, but we must show some numbers for next year, and that's your

*job. You've got a few months to assess the
situation and see what you can do. By the end
of the year I must present my budget to
Corporate, at which point I need to have your
numbers for Africa. They expect a lot of
growth, so we have to do our homework very
carefully. Just remember one very important
principle: do not promise what you cannot
deliver. My motto is:* **do what you say you will
do or don't say it.***"*

"I like that," I said, *"and I will keep it
in mind."*

*"I know you can't wait to get going. So,
tell me how you intend to get started."*

I was puzzled. Not having a clue of
what needed to be done, I had to quickly invent
something. NT had no presence at all in Africa,
none whatsoever, that's all I knew at the time.
So, I said what seemed to be the most logical
thing.

*"Well, I intend to study the market first.
I need to know where the most immediate
opportunities are."*

"Good, that's right," he said somewhat
condescendingly. *"The most immediate
opportunities are in the French-speaking
Magreb countries,"* he added with a smile.
*"You should contact the Canadian embassies
and ask them to help you set up relevant*

meetings. And if you are interested in Libya, since you were born there, you should know that we do not have an embassy in that country, but you can make appointments and travel arrangements using the embassy in Tunis. They take care of Libya as well."

That piece of information was a welcome clue. I nodded in agreement, pretending to know about it, but in fact I was green on anything concerning the Grand Magreb, other than they were former French colonies, except for Libya, and still used French rather than Arabic in all of their business dealings.

"Yes, of course," I said. "I'll send a telex immediately to the embassies in Morocco, Algeria and Tunisia. I won't bother with Libya for now. I'll start travelling as soon as they can set up meetings for me."
"I can tell you right now that you are on your own," rejoined Brian, "because no one in this office speaks French. You have been highly recommended by Hugh Hamilton and we know you are a self starter, so I am sure you will move fast. I am counting on it. If you need help from me, feel free to see me."

We continued our conversation on other subjects, especially on the English

43

lifestyle. He was a few years my senior, married to a beautiful woman, had two teen-aged boys in private school and lived in Windsor. He was proud of his Welsh origins and loved his horse, which he rode at any opportunity. He spoke clearly on what needed to be done, but was not very good at small talk. We developed a close business relationship, especially after seeing the results of my work, but he remained a 'boss', never a friend. He left me alone to handle my francophone customers, while he focused on the rich region of Saudi Arabia and the Gulf States, where he had already generated a few million dollars of business and had three in-country salesmen working full time.

ME&A was a relatively new organization, having been in business only a couple of years, and was focused entirely on selling digital PBXs of the new SL-1 line. There were only ten of us in the organization, with sales of barely $10 million. In those days the best way to communicate with developing countries was by telex messages. Even faxes were not yet available and telephone lines were either always busy or of poor quality. I sent a lengthy questionnaire to each embassy in Algiers, Rabat and Tunis. I wanted to know a lot of things about each country -- population, economic growth, size of telephone network, budget for telecom infrastructure, competing companies, loyalties, personalities and any other relevant fact of a competitive nature.

In those countries - much like anywhere else in the world other than North America - all telecommunication needs were managed by the Ministry of PTT. It made life easier for me in the sense that I had one and only one organization to deal with in each country, but it was also more difficult because of the admin red tape and various levels of management involved, and also because of their longstanding loyalties to other companies.

After a few initial meetings with technical people of the PTT, I realized that I did not have sufficient product knowledge to answer their questions, especially on the latest digital products, other than CALRS. I was actually amazed at the depth and breadth of knowledge of those engineers. They knew their stuff very well and were also courteous and well spoken.

I remember getting back home after my first trip wondering if I was the right man for the job. I had a lot to learn, not only on products but also on competitive forces. I told Brian that I needed to spend some time visiting our divisions to get a better technical understanding of our product lines. He agreed and told me to make arrangements for a two-week tour of all manufacturing facilities in Canada and the USA. That way I would not only learn the merits of our products, but I would also establish important contacts with divisional management. I wasted no time and barely a couple of months after settling in Maidenhead I was on a tour of North America. That trip gave me the technical knowledge and the confidence I needed to tackle most questions without hesitation.

As I had to communicate in French, I soon realized that I needed to improve my knowledge of the language. I struggled with business terminology, and the technical vocabulary was mostly foreign to me at that point. I therefore made a supreme effort to take notes and learn as much as I could in as short period of time as I could muster. I forced myself to read French papers and technical magazines only, and I jotted down in a pocket notebook all useful business expressions I could find.

I had to work alone in the first few months, for we had no agents and no business associates of any kind to work with. It was virgin territory for NT, dominated by the likes of Alcatel, Ericsson and Siemens. I needed to know how they operated, especially in terms of their personal relationship (payola?) with the top brass of the PTT. As I was blessed with the ability to befriend key secretaries, I managed to wine-and-dine a few and pick their brain, so to speak. I learned a lot that way, including which of our competitors were the more aggressive ones and which ones came to town with presents for key PTT employees. After a while I felt I had enough confidential information to be able to compete on an even playing field.

Brian was right when he told me that people in those countries knew little or nothing about NT and not much about Canada, which was still seen as a suburb of the US, rich in natural resources and in American culture, but poor in technology. In 1981 that notion was not too far from the truth, because Canada was still at the dawn of its technological know-how.

Based on that initial impression I made it a point to describe Canada as a bilingual French-English country with the most advanced state-of-the-art proprietary technology in North America. The idea was to play on their love for American technology but dislike for American companies. Canada was a politically neutral and friendly country, with French as one of two official languages. We could therefore provide them with French documentation, as well as training and technical support in French, something that only Alcatel could do at the time.

I worked closely with the Canadian Commercial Counselor in each country and organized technical seminars for all engineers and other technical people in the industry. A year later NT was no longer an unknown entity in the Magreb and several business opportunities popped up along the way.

In Morocco we selected and appointed Dolbeau & Fils, an influential French company with Moroccan roots, as our exclusive distributor, based in Casablanca. The first successful sale in North Africa was in Morocco. We sold a large digital PABX to the Mohammed V International Airport in Casablanca. In Tunisia we appointed a couple of agents without exclusivity, but nothing was ever accomplished in that small country. Their budget was limited and their loyalty to long-time suppliers Alcatel and Ericsson was unshakeable.

The Algerian saga

The most interesting opportunities turned out to be in Algeria. As an oil-rich country, they had the money and the need for big things in telecommunication. But Algeria was also a socialist country. The use of business intermediaries, such as representative agents and/or distributors, was illegal. Foreign companies were expected to work directly with various government agencies for all their sales contracts in Algeria.

In 1982, the year after my arrival, the country celebrated its twentieth anniversary of independence from France. To mark the event, a huge monument - *Monument aux Martyrs* -

was built in honor of their freedom fighters. The monument was financed by CIDA (Canadian International Development Agency) and was built by SNC-Lavallin, a Quebec construction company. As a result, Canada was viewed as a 'friendly francophone country', well known in Algerian government circles, something that facilitated my mission in that country. I had already had several meetings with people at different management level, but never with the Director General of the PTT. At that level, I was told, I needed the direct involvement of the Ambassador.

NT had grown considerably by then, both in Canada and the USA, but not yet in the rest of the world. It was nonetheless a major corporation and a success story in home-grown digital technology. There was therefore a lot of interest in Foreign Affairs and in all our Embassies to see NT grow in international markets and spread the Canadian high-tech brand in as many countries as possible. In other words all embassies were very helpful, at all levels, when it came to promoting NT interests. At that time Paul Laberge had just been appointed Canadian Ambassador to Algeria. He was in his late forties, very friendly, unassuming and accommodating.

I asked Don Caldwell (the Commercial Counselor) to arrange a meeting for me. Don had already done all in his power to make sure

I met with different levels of the PTT, but the Director General was out of his reach. As an anglophone Don's French was not the best, but he struggled through it with determination and usually got what he wanted. Paul Laberge, by contrast, was fully bilingual. Being new to the job, he was eager to show results, especially with an important company like NT. He met with me immediately after his arrival and offered his support. I briefed him on the situation, emphasizing the need to communicate at the highest possible levels. A few days later he arranged for me to meet with the Director General of the PTT (Monsieur Sharif).

I met M. Sharif for nearly an hour in his huge office. It was a turning point of sorts because it uncovered several important projects in which NT could play a part. I still remember Sharif's imposing personality. He was a big man, well dressed and extremely articulate. He welcomed me with a warm handshake and introduced me to Dr. Allan, his right-hand man and Chief Technologist. After the usual niceties and a cup of tea served by his obliging secretary, I started to talk about NT and told them how the company grew since its tri-corporate restructuring a dozen years earlier. A lot of questions were asked about our size, customer base, financial strength and alliances with other companies. Then, when I started to explain the advantages afforded by our technology, Sharif stopped me.

"Don't bother with the details, Monsieur Bellini," he said with some impatience. "We are familiar with the benefits, but we don't know how your system compares with those of your competitors. We are also surprised to hear that Canada has that kind of proprietary technology, so we are curious to know more. We will soon be issuing a major international tender call for 200,000 lines of digital switching, just for starters. We have already received detailed information from Alcatel, Ericsson and Siemens. If NT is interested in participating, you should bring a team of experts to give our engineers a technical seminar. Can you do so?"

I was stunned. I had to swallow hard and think quickly before responding. That was a $200 million opportunity that could not be ignored. I knew that much and I had no hesitation in confirming our interest. At the end of the meeting Dr. Allan accompanied me to the lobby and asked me some technical questions. I was surprised by the depth of his knowledge and asked him where he graduated. He told me he did his doctorate in electronic engineering at the Ecole Polytechnique in Paris (the French MIT!), one of the best in the world.

I was doubly impressed and braced myself for some very tough technical questions in future meetings.

In the evening I called Brian and briefed him. I stressed the need to arrange a visit to Algiers by a couple of technical hot shots from BNR. He was incredulous and hesitant, but also pleased. He wondered about the availability of experts, given their busy schedule and the fact that Algeria was not yet on the radar screen of corporate interests. But he agreed to give it a shot.

The next day I returned to the embassy and asked to meet again with both Don and Paul. By then they all knew me very well at the embassy and on private occasions we were on a first name basis. I remember the conversation I had with both of them in the Ambassador's office. I briefed them on my meeting and asked them what we could do to gain more visibility at top level.

"They seem to be interested in NT, but they still see Canada as trailing other countries in state-of-the-art technology," I noted. *"We need to sell them the country before we can sell them the company and the products."*

"You are right," replied Paul, *"that's why we have organized a Ministerial visit. Minister Masse and a number of Canadian*

businessmen will be here shortly on a mission to promote Canadian companies. You will be informed in due course and I expect you will join the mission as NT representative. In the meantime I could host a reception at home. In fact I am due to have one soon. I can invite many top people of interest to both NT and SNC."

"That would be fantastic," I said.

"Okay, when do you plan to be back in town?" he asked.

"I could be back in a couple of weeks."

"Why not next week?"

"It takes me a week to get a new entry visa. They are only good for one entry." I explained.

"Oh yes, of course," he said with a sigh. "We are trying to eliminate visa requirements for Canadian nationals, but it's not easy."

"Why not," I asked.

"Because they require reciprocity and we are not yet ready for that. But you are also Italian, aren't you? Don't you have an Italian passport? You don't need a visa with it."

"I have never renewed it," I said, "and I believe I lost my Italian citizenship when I acquired the Canadian one in 1973."

"You can get it back now. The laws have changed in Italy. I know it for a fact because I happen to be in Italy frequently."

"What takes you there?" I asked with curiosity.

"I own a pied-a-terre in Sorrento," he explained with a proud smile. "That's where I spend my free time. My wife lives there year-round."

I learned later that Paul was an avid sailor and owned a 32 foot fully equipped sailboat with sophisticated navigation instruments, which he used for a few Mediterranean crossings. He showed it to me one night while it was moored in Algiers. In fact we had dinner on it. We became friends by then and shared a few social evenings together, when we had nothing else to do.

Two weeks later I was one of the guests at the Ambassador's reception in his beautiful villa overlooking the harbor, on the hills of the city. He invited several top government officials from different ministries. I was introduced to various influential people, not only from the PTT, but also from Sonatrach (the oil and gas authority), and Sonatite (a special branch of the PTT in charge of small businesses). A couple of senior officers from the MOD (Ministry of Defense) were also there. By the end of the evening I had secured important business cards that proved useful in establishing strong contacts with Sonatite and Sonatrach, both of which had important needs for PBX networks. The MOD too was interested in acquiring several thousands of the latest electronic telephone sets. What followed in the next few months was a very busy time for me and for my staff in Maidenhead.

We first won our bid for an important multimillion-dollar PBX contract with Sonatrach. The communication network was to be installed all along their pipeline from various drilling sites in the desert to the city of Oran. We then won a large supply contract with Sonatite for installations in hotels, hospitals and various other small businesses around the country. Later we also won a contract with the MOD for several thousands of the latest models of electronic telephone sets, also known as POTS (Plain Ordinary Telephone Sets).

I remember a funny episode at the MOD offices when I went there to give them a few samples of the new electronics phones they had just purchased. The colonel in charge looked at those samples somewhat mystified. He lifted one, plunked it back on his desk, lifted it again and stared at me.

"This is not a phone," he said in a very serious tone of voice. "This is a toy. It's too light and too fragile."

I didn't know what to say. I remember just staring back at him dumbfounded. He then grabbed his regular and heavy black telephone set he had on his desk and plunked it back on his desk with a loud clunking sound.

"You see?" He asked rhetorically. "This is a real phone. It's solid like a rock!"

I could not help smiling, but was careful not to insult him, and explained that the electronic version did not have the heavy hardware of old phones, like ringers and transformers. They did not weigh much because it was mostly a digital device. He was not convinced and told me that they could not accept them for use in the military and that they would cancel the contract if they were not modified. I sent a telex immediately to our manufacturing division in London, Ontario, telling them of the weight problem. A few days later I received a reply in which it was recognized that the phone was indeed found to be too light by most users and that they had already added a two-pound lead base into it.

By then, Algeria alone accounted for half of all ME&A sales budget and we were well positioned to win the first tranche of a public switching tender from the PTT, worth in excess of $100 million. The need for in-country support was therefore called for.

I floated the idea at that point of establishing a technical support office in Algiers to serve the entire North African francophone region. The volume of business we had in the pipeline justified it, but it was still premature and was therefore kept under advisement.

***

Chapter Five

Cyprus

In the summer of 1983, Brian organized a brainstorming retreat for his direct reports in Cyprus. All six of us converged on the Greek part of that beautiful island with enthusiasm and optimism. There were no traces left of the 1974 armed struggle between Greeks and Turks. Turkey had already declared the northern part of the island (home to some 150,000 Turkish Cypriots) as the Turkish Republic of Northern Cyprus, and was no longer a bone of contention, even though it was never recognized by the United Nations. In the meantime the southern part held by Greek Cypriots became a very popular tourist destination and also a place for business retreats. Life was good on that island in 1983 and we all enjoyed it immensely for the duration of our stay in a great five-star hotel on the beach. Brian saw it as a way to thank his team for a lot of hard work and great results.

On that occasion I recall his initial remarks (paraphrased) at our first meeting on that island.

"I chose to get you here on this island," he said as we sat around in a small conference room, "because I want you to be away from your friends and family for a few days. I want you to clear your mind of whatever mundane problems you may have at home. I also want to say thank you for your efforts to date. We've had a good run so far, but we need to understand what to do to keep up the momentum. So, for the rest of our stay here, let's talk about ways and means to increase our revenue stream. Tell me how you see it. Think big. Think outside the box.

"I also want to say that our sales forecast for this year show that more than half of the revenue is being generated in Algeria, with contributions from Morocco and Libya. Victor has approached the market differently. He engaged the Canadian Embassy staff and, more particularly, the Canadian Ambassador to get to the top decision makers. Together they used diplomacy, relationships and a lot of persuasive technical arguments to generate huge contracts. So, let's use those diplomatic services everywhere in the Middle East. Let's cozy-up to the top decision makers in those

countries. I am sure that that's exactly what our competition is doing anyway."

I felt good at that meeting. I was at the top of my game and my confidence level could not be any higher. But something else was maturing in my persona. I was becoming conceited. Success was going to my head and a sense of infallibility took over in everything I did. I became demanding and intolerant of what I believed was the inaction of others. That attitude did not go unnoticed to Brian who called me into his office one day, closed the door and lectured me. He told me I had become too hard on my staff and also on my colleagues. He famously said something I will never forget.

"You cannot expect everyone to be as driven and proactive as you are," he told me reproachfully. "You must understand that people have different interests in life. Their career is not necessarily their only occupation. So, cut them some slack or you will end up without friends one day."

Those words hit me like a sledge hammer at first, but I was too cavalier to fully appreciate their significance. I did soften my stance from that day on, but I remained unshaken on what I expected from people I dealt with, whether on my staff or just colleagues. As a matter of fact, contrary to some ambitious colleagues I worked with, I was not an egomaniac. I never used the pronoun 'I' in any of my reports. I used 'we' and always gave credit to where credit was due. But I was overly critical of underperforming individuals, especially of those who promised a lot and delivered very little.

In the meantime my weekly activity reports (known as WARs) were being copied to and read by the upper management in Canada. They gave me visibility and increased popularity.

Under my leadership North Africa became the most valuable markets for ME&A. The business volume was such that it required the opening of an office in Algiers, with local and expatriate staff. We needed to install equipment, train local staff, provide technical support and keep a continuous line of communication with our customers. We were also starting to negotiate the terms and conditions for a transfer of technology and local manufacturing of our DMS product line. It was a process that required a lot of interaction with our Algerian counterpart on technical, management and legal matters.

Brian felt it was his responsibility to take part in the early negotiations and promotional activities for those big projects, but did not speak a word of French and felt like a fish out of waters. One day he told me he was determined to learn the language. I told him it takes time to learn a new language from scratch, but he disagreed. He signed up for a full immersion course in Paris for a whole month. Well, it did not help much and eventually he gave up.

The early part of those negotiations in Algeria and Morocco was therefore entirely my show and required a strong in-country presence, with a full time manager and office staff. I reminded Brian of what we discussed earlier and showed him a plan detailing the economics of a support office in Algiers. He was skeptical at first but eventually agreed and gave me the go-ahead.

I rented a large three-storey house in a convenient downtown location and had it converted into office space downstairs and an apartment upstairs for my personal use. I then bought a car (Peugeot 505), hired a driver, a maid, a secretary (an Algerian young lady called Zara), and an office manager from France (Jacques Cadro). I also made arrangements for a team of French-speaking engineers from our Canadian divisions for a two-year stint as expats in Algeria. More staff was hired locally as needed to help with installation activities in the desert. I was appointed General Manager (grade 17), with full P&L responsibilities, and a budget exceeding $20 million to start with, more than half of all ME&A in the 1985 fiscal year.

In the meantime office activities in Algiers had increased to the point that my presence there was required nearly full time. My relocation to Algiers was therefore suggested. However, residing in Algiers - a French-Arabic speaking country - with an English-speaking wife and three children in the English school system, was not a desirable option for me, nor was it an option to leave the family in Maidenhead and be away from home for long periods.

An acceptable compromise was to live in Rome, just an hour flight away from Algiers, and commute weekly, which enabled me to spend every weekend with the family. It also made sense financially, given the exorbitant cost of renting acceptable living accommodation in Algiers. Travelling back and forth on a weekly basis was not uncommon among senior executives working abroad and it didn't seem to bother anyone in the company. So, in agreement with the family, I accepted to move to Rome, with a lot of excitement and an invigorating sense of adventure.

Libya

In parallel with the French Magreb, I also managed to crack the market in Libya, Kenya and Senegal. I recall my first trip to Tripoli as a businessman in 1982. I was very excited to have a chance to return to the place where I grew up. I used my Canadian passport to avoid being recognized as a former colonialist by hostile hard liners. Hotel reservations were usually made and confirmed by telex in 1982. When I arrived at the hotel in Tripoli I was told that the room was no longer available and that my telex was useless. Other business people were treated in like manner and were all standing or sitting around in the lobby, trying to figure out where to go for a room. I joined them and used the hotel phone to contact my host, Mohamed Naily, a senior executive at the NTC (National Telecom Company).

He told me he would send a driver to pick me up and drive me to their own hotel in town, compliment of NTC. I was glad for the offer, but not for long. It turned out that their hotel, rated 3-star, was in fact the filthiest place I had ever set foot in. The en-suite toilet had not been washed in ages and was caked with excrements. I quickly opened the window in the bathroom to air it out and closed the door to minimize its smell. I was demoralized and could not contemplate staying in that dump for two solid days.

Unfortunately I had no other option and had to put up with it. I decided not eat or drink anything for the duration of my stay, as a way to avoid having to use the toilet. The bed too didn't look inspiring, as the sheets appeared to have been slept in. I therefore stretched my raincoat on the blanket and slept on it in my clothes. Those were the two longest and toughest days of my life, but resulted in an excellent business opportunity.

A few months later I returned to Tripoli and was pleasantly surprised to stay at an excellent hotel on the harbor, ran by Swiss staff. In the intervening period, in fact, four new hotels had been opened, in time for a major yearly convention of the OAS (Organization of African States), which was presided by Gheddafi (it was his turn).

I finalized the terms and conditions for a major contract on that trip with an unwritten agreement on price and commission sealed by handshake. The actual paper contract was agreed to be negotiated and signed a couple of weeks later in my Maidenhead office by a young engineer appointed by NTC. He would be unaware of our tacit agreement, which included a commission to be deposited in a Swiss bank account. The idea was to make it look all above board, and give the engineer a feeling of achievement at being able to bring the contract price down to the level he was authorized to. I didn't mind playing the game and I enjoyed stretching it to the limit. When we finally signed the agreement I could see a big smile of satisfaction on the engineer's face. I was happy for him, but he didn't know he had been used.

I took the opportunity on that second trip to revisit on long walks the places of my youth, expecting to relive some of the exhilarating moments I remembered so vividly, but much to my chagrin things had changed. Libya was no longer an Italian colony and Tripoli was no longer the city I left eighteen years earlier. The coup d'état by Gheddafi in 1969 resulted in the repatriation en masse of all Italian nationals, a fact that changed forever the character and physiognomy of the city.

Gone were many of the elegant shops located along major boulevards; gone were the lush gardens in main piazzas and the oleander shrubs adorning the 'corsos' (main streets); and gone was the cross on the cathedral which was converted into a mosque. I walked and reminisced all over town and a few hours later I was back at the hotel, disappointed by what I had seen, but also conscious of the fact that the Libyans were building their own country to their own needs and liking. They deserved a chance after so many centuries of foreign domination.

Kenya

Another experience worth reflecting upon took place in Nairobi, Kenya in 1983. I was in that city for a seminar, as I had done in other countries. I checked into the Sheraton downtown in the evening and decided to take a quick walk after dinner, before retiring for the night. Judging from the window of the hotel, the city streets looked interesting, well lit and crowded with people. I took a map from the concierge and walked out, eager to see what they had to sell in the shops. Before long I was accosted by two black men in their twenties, one at one side and one at the other. They introduced themselves as university students and, with very friendly manners, asked me where I was from and other personal questions, as if we were good friends.

A few minutes later I began to feel uncomfortable and started to look for an excuse to get away, but they stayed very close to me and eventually asked me if I could provide them with financial assistance to help pay for their studies. At that point I knew for sure I was in trouble. I played dumb and continued to look around for an escape route. A group of Caucasian tourists with a guide at the other side of the street looked like what I was looking for. I jumped away from them and ran across the street to join the tourist group. They looked stunned and angry at losing me, but there was nothing they could do.

The following morning, during my meeting with the Commercial Counselor at the Canadian embassy, I told the story and learned that I was lucky to get away from a robbery and probably also a beating. Those guys were known to be mostly, but not only, youths from Uganda who attacked Caucasian business people for money. They also attacked young women walking alone for sex. What was most disturbing about it was the fact that they seemed to get away with such crimes unscathed.

In the afternoon, at a technical seminar I gave to managers and engineers of the PTT, I was favorably impressed with their educational level. They behaved professionally and showed interest and good manners, but appeared to keep their distance. I found that attitude strange, given the fact that I represented an important western company offering free (CIDA-financing was like a gift) technology they badly needed.

At the end of the seminar, I was invited by the VP of Procurement to an exclusive country club for dinner. I was driven there in his large Mercedes (all important people drove

Mercedes cars in that country). He was a jovial and talkative individual, who ignored all stop signs while crossing city streets. He must have noticed my discomfort at his driving style and assured me that I had nothing to worry about, because he had the right of way with a bigger and better car. He laughed it off, of course, but I didn't find it reassuring.

The following evening I had dinner with the Commercial Counselor at his house, a walled-in villa in the suburbs. I learned that foreign expats living in Nairobi had to have defensive means against marauding young criminals, who attacked in droves and robbed whatever they could. It didn't happen often, but it did happen to many people.

Foreign diplomats and businessmen living in that city had to have guard dogs and a security guard at their residences (usually single villas), along with a safe room in which to hide in case of an invasion. What a way to live, I thought to myself; and yet, most expatriates were willing to renew their two-year contracts for longer stays. There certainly was an inexplicable amount of magic in that continent that I found fascinating. It was impossible to understand and appreciate their lifestyle without actually living there.

Senegal

Much as I liked to feel the 'magic' of black Africa during my travels to the Eastern part of the continent, I was emotionally overwhelmed by the people and the music of the Western part of Africa. Senegal was amazing from a human point of view. I walked the streets of Accra and talked to several people at random; they all expressed themselves in perfect French. Whether in shops or just sitting on sidewalks carving little wooden statuettes for tourists, they were humble and courteous.

There was no anger or resentment of any kind on their faces. They had an expression of satisfaction, seemingly content with their life, as if it was the best possible. Men and women alike moved about, or sat in coffee bars, or tended their shops with kindness and a sense of duty. It might have been just an impression, but I had the distinct feeling that there was a definite difference in attitude between indigenous black people from the East and the West.

In Nairobi I saw aggressive and ambitious people walking the streets, with clear and unabashed disregard and even disrespect for Caucasian foreigners, to the point where it was unsafe to walk alone in the evening. Not so in Accra. I felt perfectly safe going for a stroll in the evening all by myself. I wondered whether that difference was the result of two colonizing approaches; from England in the East and from France in the West. On the one hand I saw aggressive and confrontational people, while on the other I saw them as tolerant and accommodating.

I was in Senegal and Cameroon for two days of talks with the PTT of each country, and for technical seminars with their managers and engineers. I found their questions to be on par with the professional level of their counterparts in Nairobi. They were all eager to know about the latest technology had to offer, but were also cognizant of the fact that they could not afford much of what was available.

In the evening of my last day there, I had dinner in a most colorful open-air restaurant in the back patio of the Hilton hotel. I sat there long after my dinner companion left and enjoyed a cognac while listening to the music of a local group. I cannot describe the emotional impact that music had on me. It was more like a lament, almost a prayer-like melody, sang with feeling and abandon. It flowed in a continuous stream of music and lyrics beautifully blended together.

It being a Friday night, there were quite a few people in the restaurant, mostly natives of social and financial means. They all seemed to take that music for granted, as if it was normal run of the mill. But to my ears, that music had an angelic element to it. As I left the restaurant I approached their leader and asked him where I could buy a tape of their music. He laughed and told me that there were no recordings. He then added that they were playing well known tribal songs, adapted to a different beat.

As I walked back to my room I remembered an aphorism I knew from Italy, a country where many people in menial jobs sing opera arias or popular songs while they work. They can be women doing their chores at home or men sweating it out on construction sites.

The aphorism says that there are too many famous singers who should be bricklayers, and too many bricklayers who should be professional singers. It's an exaggeration, to be sure, but there is an element of truth in it, and those musicians in Accra are prime examples of what uncelebrated talent is all about.

Chapter Six

Fast growth in all markets

By 1985, thanks to its superior digital technology, NT managed to assert itself internationally and grew exponentially, especially in the USA, but also in Asia, Europe and the ME&A. It employed well over forty thousand people, with revenues exceeding six billion dollars, and was well positioned for further growth. The digital family of products, DMS *in primis*, had made the company a powerhouse in North America and a fast growing concern elsewhere.

At that junction Ben Beneteau, as President of NT-International, was a bit of a prima donna with big ideas and a big ego. But to my surprise he turned out to be my mentor and was instrumental in placing my territory on NTI priority list. As a bilingual French-English man, Ben had a weakness for North African countries, especially for Algeria, Morocco and Libya, where I had already signed multimillion dollar contracts. He saw great opportunities in those markets for major public switching

73

contracts and gave me unlimited support for my efforts. In the case of Libya, he knew that I was born in that country and that I had already signed a multimillion dollar contract for digital concentrators of the new DMS-1 family. He saw it as an opening for a special project he had in mind.

By 1985 Libya had become an oil rich country, with revenues exceeding Gheddafi's wildest dreams, and was engaged in massive infrastructural activities involving major international contractors. One of those contractors was Daewoo, a huge South Korean trading corporation involved in a variety of business ventures around the world, and also in manufacturing activities in Korea, including cars under license from GM and consumer electronics.

In Libya Daewoo was one of the larger contractors for buildings and road construction and employed in excess of two thousand people, mostly brought in from Korea. The company was led by Chairman Kim, a visionary and entrepreneur par excellence, known to be a workaholic who practically lived on his personal jet, as he moved constantly from country to country to drum up new business ventures. He built Daewoo from zero to a seven billion dollar corporation in less than ten years!

Chairman Kim had initiated negotiations with NT for a license to manufacture digital PBX of the SL1 family in Seoul and was therefore well acquainted with Ben Beneteau. It was during one of their meetings that Ben came to appreciate Daewoo strength in Libya and proposed that the two companies study the possibility of joining forces for an ambitious project, aimed at rebuilding the entire Libyan telephone network, known to be in urgent need of expansion.

Ben thought that we had a strong case to make to the Libyans as joint bidders and persuaded Chairman Kim to organize a trip to Tripoli to explore the possibilities. The trip was made in mid-summer on Chairman Kim private jet and consisted of Kim, Ben, Dr. Park (Daewoo GM of its electronics division), Kim's secretary and myself. Ben came equipped with a carousel of slides intended as a presentation to the Minister of Telecom and asked me to be prepared to discuss potential technical solutions.

We took off from London and landed in Tripoli in early afternoon. Chairman Kim had a telex with a confirmed appointment with the Minister of Telecom for a meeting to be held the following morning at the Ministry. Upon landing we were welcomed in style by a couple of individuals who loaded our luggage on a trolley and escorted us to the VIP lounge for passport formalities. We handed in our passports and waited in comfortable surroundings, including a choice of free unalcoholic drinks.

A few minutes later we were confronted by an unfriendly young man of obvious authority who demanded to know who the leader of our delegation was. As Chairman Kim stood silent and dumbfounded, Ben volunteered that he was the leader, at which point he became the target of a hostile tirade from the young man who accused Ben of wanting to enter the country under false pretenses. Ben was flabbergasted and looked around at all of us wondering what was going on. The young man went on telling us in insulting language that their 'leader' had no meeting scheduled with us and that therefore we made it all up.

After realizing that by 'leader' he meant Gheddafi, Kim's secretary explained that our meeting was with the Minister of Telecom, not with Gheddafi, and showed a telex as proof. At that point the young man calmed down and angrily told us that we were not VIPs and that we should line up at passport control like all other passengers. We shook our heads in disbelief and meekly walked to the other side of the terminal, dragging our luggage behind us. Ben could hardly refrain from giving that young man a tirade of his own, but he didn't. He told us later that he had a strong urge to punch the guy (Ben was a pugilist in is young days).

We eventually checked into our hotel in Tripoli and went for a tour of Daewoo construction site and administrative offices, fully fenced-in and guarded. The organization was impressive, as was the way they treated their Korean employees. They were all housed and fed on site in a series of prefab homes and a large canteen. A more formal dining room was also available for management and that's where we dined and talked.

Upon returning to the hotel, Ben gave me his carousel of slides and asked me to do the presentation to the Minister and his entourage the next morning. He preferred to sit with the Minister to answer whatever questions he may have had. I was shocked. I didn't even know what was in his carousel, let alone present it to high ranking authorities.

Later in the evening, in my hotel room, I spent over an hour checking every slide through a table lamp (I did not have a projector) and took some notes. Luckily the presentation was just a standard corporate one, detailing the company history, accomplishments and product line, something I knew very well.

The following morning we met at the Minister's offices and I was introduced by Ben as a former Libyan native, having been born and schooled there (in Italian). The Minister was very surprised and addressed me in Arabic, asking me where I was born. I did speak enough to understand and make myself understood, so I answered his question but quickly added that I did not speak well enough for a formal conversation. He laughed and switched to Italian, a language he spoke well, and told me with a smile that I was welcome back in the country even though I was an ex colonialist!

At that point Ben was lost and jokingly begged us to use English so they could all understand what was going on. That incident broke the ice and made my presentation more relaxed and very well received. Chairman Kim was impressed and asked if I was available to eventually lead the telecom team in country. I replied in no uncertain terms that I would be pleased to do whatever work I could for the project, but not in Libya. As it turned out, the project never materialized and a couple of years later we learned that Daewoo was no longer active in Libya.

By then, Ben communicated directly with me on many occasions regarding my activities in the French Magreb. Brian didn't like that, but because of linguistic problems he tolerated it and did not interfere. Ben was interested in winning the big switching contract in Algeria and a similar one in Morocco. He wanted to be kept abreast of everything I was doing.

The trip to Libya marked a turning point for me. I had stepped up into senior management circles and was wallowing in success. I had a direct link to the President and was well known at all levels of NT International. I reported on business activities at senior meetings in Toronto on several occasions. I was welcomed and respected in any business event of relevance, such as conferences and seminars where NT presented papers and participated in ministerial delegations.

I was invited to be part of the Switching Symposium in Florence, Italy, where I took my wife and stayed a few days at the Baglioni Hotel, a five-star hotel in central Florence. I was also invited to participate and speak at a Telecom Show and conference in Geneva, and one in Versailles. In other words, I was flying high and ignored whatever cold shoulder I was getting from Brian.

It was probably Ben's doing that got me signed up for a one-week course in Ireland on executive management. The course was all about organizational skills, financial management, and crisis management. We were only four Directors at my level on the course, and we were clearly being groomed for higher management. On the last day we played the role of the CEO of a public company and were provided with the summary of a fictitious corporation operating on the brink of bankruptcy. We were given a few hours to study the case and ask pertinent questions (to test our analytical abilities). We were then given an afternoon - working independently in our own room - to propose a plan to save the company from an impending bankruptcy.

The four plans were then presented by each 'trainee' in bullet form on a set of transparencies to a panel of senior executives, including Ben and Brian. To prevent unnecessary expectations for quick promotions, the results of that test were never officially revealed, but it was clear to me from the demeanor and countenance of the examiners that I did very well. I therefore knew I was slated for bigger things.

A couple of months later I was appointed General Manager for North Africa while retaining my other duties as Director of Business Development for the rest of Africa. I was given full authority to lead a team of experts engaged in negotiating the T&Cs of a major public switching contract with the Algerian PTT.

To help me out in that mission I took a course on International Contract Law in Amsterdam. The attendees were from all over Europe and included senior managers of different corporations. I found the course very revealing and informative and benefited from it immensely but, more than that, it gave me an exaggerated sense of self-worth which bordered on arrogance. I felt I knew it all, I could do no wrong and was ready to challenge anyone who disagreed with me, at any level. That kind of arrogance added to my strength with my subordinates but it did not endear me to my colleagues, and it eventually hurt my career. I wish I knew then what I know now about the drawbacks of being arrogant. A bit of humility at any level of authority is a virtue that should be better appreciated.

As business opportunities heated up in 1986 Ben instigated a tour of North Africa in a private jet that included himself, as President of NTI, Ray Cyr as President of Bell Canada, Brian Baynes as Managing Director of ME&A and myself as General Manager for North Africa. He inadvertently announced the plan directly to me rather than to Brian. He invited our wives to go along. Brian felt sidelined and had his nose out of joint for a while. He told me that he would not bring his wife on the tour and that I should not bring my wife either, but I refused, arguing that it was Ben himself who invited me.

From that point on my relationship with Brian became frosty. I was wrong to have snubbed him and I was wrong in being brash and cocky with him, but in my defense I saw no reason why he should object to the presence of our wives. I learned later that he was having marital problems at the time and did not feel comfortable taking his wife along. Be it as it may, he took my 'disobedience' very badly and made no bones about it, but I was too sure of myself to worry about minor disagreements. I was flying high as a top performer and felt good in my skin.

The tour took us to Rabat, Casablanca, Algiers, Tlemcen and Tunis. In Tlemcen (Algeria) we visited a plant slated to be converted to a digital manufacturing facility with DMS equipment, a project worth well over $100 million. Signing that contract would have been a ground-breaker for NT, for it would have made it a major competitor in the region where other countries were actively considering going digital. It would also have created a template for opportunities in Europe, including one in Italy with Telecom Italia, then known as STET.

In fact, soon after the tour, Ben invited me to Canada to present to his Cabinet an update on Algeria and Morocco and an action plan. Brian was not invited. Ben knew that Brian's lack of French made him a non player in francophone Africa and that's why he dealt with me directly (and did so in French when we were alone, for he loved to speak it, even though English was his mother tongue).

That session with Ben's Cabinet resulted in another assignment for me. I was asked to contact Italtel (the NT of Italy) and STET in Rome to assess their potential interest in a business association with NT. The aim was to spread the use of digital DMS technology, whether by direct sales or by technology transfer. At that time Italtel was developing its own digital switch but did not yet have a working system. I was seen as the perfect person to do the introductory work because I spoke Italian fluently and lived in Rome.

My first meeting with STET included the Canadian Commercial Counselor who insisted on an official Canadian presence to add importance and credibility. I was also asked to avoid communicating in Italian if at all possible. As it happened, the DG of STET spoke excellent English and the meeting was therefore conducted in that language, except during a coffee break.

The interest shown by STET in associating with NT was very serious and was so relayed to Ben and his cabinet. In a subsequent memo Ben requested that I take the lead in Italy and arrange for a top level meeting at the earliest opportunity. I did so, but two meetings later I was told that the Zurich office would do the follow ups and that Ben Beneteau would no longer be involved. That event signaled the beginning of the end of my run to the top as my mentor was being sidelined.

Truth be told though, the assignment of the job to the Zurich office made sense from an organizational point of view, given that the Italian market was a purview of NT-Europe, based in Zurich. It made sense on paper, except that I was the one who started the ball rolling, and I was the one who spoke the language flawlessly and was intimately familiar with the technology. I was disappointed, of course, but the move turned out to be part of a major reorganization at all levels of the corporation, including the appointment of a new CEO.

***

Chapter Seven

Organizational changes

In late 1986 major changes started to take place at the top of the company. Ben Beneteau was replaced as President of NT-International by Bob Ferchat, a financial guy and former executive from the Ford Motor Company. Ben was moved out of a job he did exceedingly well for less than three years. He was of retirement age and was appointed Vice Chairman of the holding company -- an honorific title with no powers. He took it in stride and made it sound like a promotion, but in fact he was being sidelined.

In domino-effect style, Bob Ferchat appointed Bruce Tavner, a former VP from Bell Canada, to replace Hugh Hamilton as President of NT-Europe, and Bruce brought on board Charlie Baker, a close friend of his also from Bell Canada, to replace Brian Baynes as Managing Director of ME&A.

The reorganization was prompted by a new CEO, Paul Stern - a narcissistic megalomaniac from the USA. Paul was supposed to take the company to bigger and better things all over the world, but ended up taking it down to near financial collapse. He was fired less than three years into the job. In the meantime the damage was done.

On hearing the news that Ben was out I saw red, as did most of my colleagues. I can understand the desire of a new CEO to bring his own team of trusted colleagues on board, but I do not understand why proven executives with years of international experience and personal connections were suddenly replaced with people who had hardly ever traveled outside their own country. Bruce's international experience was to manage a large project Bell had in Saudi Arabia. That was it. As to Charlie, my new boss, he was as green as anything, not only on international affairs, but also on product lines.

Other management changes took place in all other parts of the company as the corporate mission changed its set of priorities. Paul Stern, the incoming CEO, perhaps because of his American upbringing, decided to make the USA a 'strategic' market, where most of the investments in R&D and market development would be focused. The international arena became 'opportunistic', in the sense that marketing efforts and technology development necessary to meet international standards would be undertaken if and only if there were immediate opportunities of substantial long-term value.

It was the considered opinion of many of us on the sidelines that something else was in the making, and that a good dose of nepotism or any other form of favoritism was at play. Such is the game being played at the top of corporate management that it's not always obvious why changes are made. Be it as it may, with Ben gone, Bob Ferchat found himself on a long learning curve, while Bruce Tavner struggled, and Charlie Baker was just a clueless character close to retirement.

It's a well known fact that some managers, at any level, who happen to have bright individuals on their staff, worry about being replaced by one of them. This reality hit me when Tavner appointed his loyal friend Charlie Baker to replace Brian Baynes. Tavner found himself in uncharted territory and worried about being manipulated by too many experienced and smart people in his new administration. He therefore chose to have a protective buffer zone, so to speak, of loyal friends as his direct reports. In so doing he created confusion not only at staff level, but also and primarily with important customers.

There were two senior people that should have been considered to replace Brian Baynes: Hans Diemel and Victor Bellini -- we both expected to be approached. To our surprise and chagrin, however, we were never considered and when we asked for an explanation we were told that we did not have the necessary 'visibility'. It was a lame explanation, for Hans and I were both star performers and had very strong visibility at all levels of NTI management in those days.

With Brian gone, Charlie was the man to cozy up to and Bruce Tavner as the next in line before getting to Bob Ferchat. I felt cheated. From having a direct link with the President of NTI, I was essentially pushed down two levels. It didn't affect my grade, but my influence and prestige had taken a hit.

Brian Baynes was quickly pushed out of his large office and given a small office to sit in as he looked for another job within NTI. It was a very sad case. In hindsight, I should have shown empathy and understanding, but I didn't. I remember a comment Brian made during a casual chat we had over a beer at the pub. He looked angry and despondent.

"It's incredible how fast allegiances can change in business," he lamented. *"You are at the top one day and at the bottom the next. And yet, you are the same person!"*

The comment was generic in nature but, in retrospect, it was also addressed to me, because I failed to show any understanding for his predicament and remained the cocky person I had become.

"What prompted this sudden change?"
I asked. "Did you know it was coming?"

"I did know that a new CEO would want to have his own team," he replied, "but none of us expected a domino effect like this. It's too quick, too soon."

"It will surely disrupt a lot of personal relationships with our customers," I submitted.

"Yes, that's a given. This guy, Paul Stern, is a bit of a prima donna. He acts like he knows it all already, with swagger and self-importance. He should have taken time to understand the business we have created and the people who made it happen. We have been the fastest growing company in our field for years, and this guy thinks we are a bunch of morons."

"Your successor, Charlie Baker, ahm,"
I asked tongue in cheek, "how well do you know him? He looks a bit flaky to me."

"Hmm," he scoffed, "good luck with him! I don't know him at all, but he worked for Bruce at Bell and they have been friends for a long time. I suppose that Bruce is worried about loyalty from people like me. What a farce!"

"I am very disappointed as well," I said softly. *"I expected to at least be considered for the job. I thought that it would be either me or Hans to take over from you, but neither one of us has been approached."*

"Well, don't look at me! Nobody asked for my opinion. I wish you good luck, but if I were you I would start looking for a job back in Canada. The company has grown a lot and has a lot of talented people available locally. Expats are no longer needed."

"Hans and I are the only expats in senior positions in Maidenhead," I observed.

"Hans already told me that he will stay here as a local employee. As you know, he has no children and his wife has an art studio in London, plus, he is Dutch, so ... his home is in Europe."

"In other words I am the only one left as expat besides Charlie. Should I start packing my bags?"

"You are still safe for a year or so because there is no francophone ready to replace you, but watch out. You will soon have to make a choice."

After that conversation I was fuming with anger. As the company grew, so did senior management levels. Consequently the making of fast decisions became a thing of the past. Strangely enough, though, I never felt threatened in those days. I was convinced that my management level at grade 17 would quickly place me in an equivalent position as Group Director and maybe even give me an upgrade. I was sure that it was just a matter of time before I would be a VP somewhere in the international organization.

A few months later, Hans accepted to stay in London as a local employee, while I chose to stay longer as an expat and waited for better times to come my way.

The appointment of Charlie as Managing Director didn't make any sense. He was unqualified in every sense of the word and soon proved to be a square peg in a round hole. He had a hard time understanding the issues and was slow in making decisions, which were often forced on him. His appointment raised a lot of questions and malicious rumors about Bruce himself.

Contrary to Ben Beneteau, neither Charlie nor Bruce showed any interest in North Africa, most likely because they did not speak a word of French. All market initiatives I recommended slowed down to a crawl and often failed to materialize for lack of interest. Technical resources for important negotiations on transfer of technology (part of our switching bids) were never made available, allegedly because needed in more important markets.

Eventually Morocco turned away from NT and focused on Alcatel for their digital switches, while Algeria was still very much in bed with us, but lamented the lack of aggressive activity. To stir things up I organized a trip to Canada and the USA for the DG of the PTT and the DG of their manufacturing plant in Tlemcen. They were both very sharp and knowledgeable men with engineering degrees.

We were in the middle of negotiating the switching contract – a $200 million job - and their strong desire to visit our labs and talk to our designers was indicative of their strong preference for our equipment. I made the arrangements with excitement and with great expectations. I made it clear in a memo to Charlie, with copies to Bruce Tavner and Bob Ferchat, that Algeria was essentially in the bag and that we should make sure we treated those two top decision makers with the utmost attention and due respect in three locations -- in Ottawa for talks with BNR, and in Bramalea and Raleigh (NC) for an appreciation of our manufacturing facilities.

As it turned out, we were very well received by John Roth, President of BNR, and his staff. (As an aside, it's worth noting that John became the CEO of NTL a few years later. He provoked its demise with expensive acquisitions in the hay days of 1998-99).

The Bramalea people also did a good job, but in Raleigh it was a disaster. We were snubbed by the top management who ignored the visit as if we were nobodies. I complained and had very harsh words for their management, something for which I was later rebuked, but the incident showed the arrogance of the US team and their total lack of interest in Middle East business.

Dr. Allan, who headed the negotiating team of the PTT, was impressed with BNR and the manufacturing facilities in Bramalea, but he was bitterly disappointed with Raleigh. He told me he was not surprised at their arrogance because that's the way American companies were viewed in his country. He and I became friends after that trip. He later told me in confidence that the contract was ours if we agreed to play ball. The allusion to a secret financial transaction was obvious, but was never officially verbalized.

Not long thereafter it became obvious that NT had lost interest in North Africa, as they were totally focused on a US market that was growing by leaps and bounds and represented 60% of all NTL sales. What they did not consider was the fact that our share of the US market was close to saturation, while the rest of the world continued to grow at a healthy pace.

In tandem with those sentiments, political restlessness began to show up in Algeria, as new elections seemed to be in favor of the Muslim Brotherhood party. As a result, NT got cold feet and dropped the ball completely. I was told to stop all further activities for public switching in both Algeria and Morocco, and just continue to manage existing contracts. It was the beginning of the end and I was furious. After years of dedicated work and after getting so close to one of the most important contracts NT had ever signed, I was told to drop it! I remember the expression of incredulity from Dr. Allan (he had replaced M. Sharif as DG of the Algerian PTT), when I broke the news. He couldn't believe it and told me bluntly that NT was by far the favorite to win the bid.

I tried to change that decision at NTI, but to no avail. Bruce told me in no uncertain terms that the decision was made at the highest level (that's Paul Stern!) and was irrevocable. The official explanation was that the corporation did not want to venture into political unrest, and that NT was way overloaded with growth in the US and Asia, where Japan and South Korea had become major customers and, in some cases, also licensees. But to me that explanation was a personal affront, a repudiation of my work, and it hurt. I did not take it kindly and I might have ruffled some feathers with some of my more acerbic comments.

As I reflect back on those years in Europe I feel cathartic and somewhat guilty. In my last year there, I was on top of the world. I had it all and was supremely confident in my abilities, but I never made any effort to understand and play the political game.

In the upper middle management of a large multinational corporation we all have the ability to manage people, manage financial matters, understand market needs, write aggressive business plans and create the conditions for long-term strategies. We are all equally capable of budgeting and forecasting. For those of us involved in international operations, we had the added advantage of having a more complete picture of addressable markets, competitive forces, product evolution, consumer's needs and cultural differences.

But at that level, the prerequisites for higher places are not just based on management ability, but also on questionable personal attributes, such as sycophantic yes-man acquiescence. Loquacious people (the talkers and advertisers) have a decisive advantage, while reflective ones (the thinkers and doers) are at a distinct disadvantage.

That political game is not for everyone. It requires a special nose and social skills to be at the right place at the right time, and say the right thing to the right people. There is only so much room at the top, that's why it's important to have thick skin and play the game, no matter how unpleasant it may be. Some people, like me, with pride and dignity, are simply not capable and not willing to play that game. I had therefore become cynical, arrogant and blasé, or so I was told.

Despite all the drawbacks, however, I never ever thought I would one day leave Nortel for greener pastures. I made my bones in that company. I grew up in lockstep with it and matured together, from humble beginnings to multinational pride and success. I had proven my technical and management worth in global environments beyond all doubts. I therefore expected to continue to contribute to the growth of the company in one form or another, whether in Europe or elsewhere.

Well, from that point on things did not evolve exactly the way I expected. The company I had come to appreciate and love as an employee-friendly institution that helped me so much in the beginning, had changed into an arrogant organization for which quick profit, backstabbing, turf battles, parochialism and nepotism were the new imperatives. Open long-term relationships based on merit, whether with employees or customers, were no longer required. A case in point was the despicable way NT treated Algeria. It was like a bride being jilted at the altar.

***

Chapter Eight

Back in North America

In early 1987, as expected, all remaining expats, except Bruce and Charlie, were told to prepare for repatriation to our original location -- Toronto in my case. I was offered a choice between repatriation and a position as a local employee in charge of the Italian market, reporting to the Zurich office. I saw it as a demotions, even though I would have retained my management grade. Furthermore, as a local employee I would have been on a local salary, commensurate with other Italian managers at my level, without expat benefits. I considered it at first and I would have accepted to stay in Rome but family considerations and career potential made me decide otherwise. I thought I would be better off in Canada where my boys were born and agreed to go back in July. Much as it had happened to Brian I did not have a specific job and was told to make the necessary inquiries for job opportunities at my management level.

Only then I appreciated what Brian had gone through and prepared myself for a shock. In fact, I was told over and over again by human resources that at my management level it would be difficult to find a position in Canada or the USA because I lacked North America experience. What a pile of crap! The real reason was that job openings were limited at that level, and there was a clear dislike for expats coming back to take senior jobs they did not grow into or compete for.

The phenomenon was well known and was also written about and debated in business magazines, as it affected not just NTI but also other multinationals around the world. Re-integrating expats in the national organization proved difficult in the best of times. To make things worse, North America was suffering from a period of low economic growth in 1987, and the management changes imposed by Paul Stern were sputtering along, with less than stellar results. In other words, the company was not doing well. So I expected the worst.

Life in Miami

A couple of agonizing months after being back in Toronto, I was offered a position with CALA (Caribbean and Latin America) in Miami, as Senior Director of Business Development, reporting to the President (Emile Gratton), a francophone Quebecer with knowledge of Spanish. My job was to open the doors to our products in Latin America, starting with Mexico, where we had no presence at all. I was expected to move to Miami, but moving the family again a few months after having resettled back in Toronto was a non-starter for several reasons. I had just purchased a larger house, needed to accommodate a growing family and all our furniture, including what we brought from Rome. My first son started his university education in Waterloo and my other two sons had been enrolled in local high schools. As well, Mary's mother - an octogenarian living alone with her son in Toronto - deserved to have her daughter and grand children close by in the last few years of her life. She had been deprived of their presence for six years already and it didn't seem fair to abandon her again at that time.

Moving to Miami was therefore out of the question, and I chose to again travel weekly back and forth, from my Toronto office to offices in Miami and in Mexico City. Once on the job, I wasted no time to start my business development activities with Telmex, the Mexican telephone authority. I was also primed in Spanish, a language so close to Italian and French that I had no problem understanding and that I knew I could learn quickly. I had a local engineer (Geraldo Gonzales) as my assistant in a small shared office in Mexico City. Geraldo worked hard to establish a rapport with several key people in Telmex and other private companies. He organized meetings, did translations, acted as my interpreter and did follow-ups. He was a good man, technically competent and well organized.

The Mexican market in those days was still not quite open for business and had to be treated differently. Mexico, like China and Brazil, was not a signatory of the GATT agreement (later known as World Trade Organization) and did not therefore comply with international trade agreements. They required foreign suppliers to export from Mexico as much as they wanted to import into Mexico, which forced foreign companies to engage in some countertrade activities, or establish manufacturing facilities in Mexico and create value-added exports. Contrary to some other multinationals, NT had never been involved in countertrade and would therefore find it difficult to consider that option. Establishing manufacturing activities was therefore the only viable alternative. I recommended that approach and engaged in a detailed analysis of the possibilities. A few months later I produced a strategic plan and presented it to Emile for approval.

Mexico had some very active free-trade zones along the US border, known as Maquilladoras. We saw an opportunity for a win-win plan that would establish assembly plants in Mexico to produce labor-intensive products and thereby generate exports to counterbalance imports of our digital products.

We identified two struggling assembly plants ideally suited to a move -- one was in Montreal and the other in Chicago. They produced cable harnesses and connectors, employing close to five hundred unionized unskilled workers, at an average cost of some twenty dollars an hour, fully absorbed. We could move such operations to Mexico and do the same job at less than five dollars an hour, also fully absorbed.

The result of such move would be a more competitive product at much lower cost, and the generation of substantial exports from Mexico which would enable sales of telecom equipment to Telmex. The plan made a lot of sense but was not easy to implement, for two reasons. First we had to close down two plants and fight it out with unions in both Canada and the USA. And then we had to find reliable partners in Mexico to help with the red tape in setting up Maquilladora operations. A decision was eventually made to go for it and a team of legal and accounting experts was then created to make it happen.

In parallel with Mexico, but at a lower priority level, I also studied markets and produced preliminary plans for Argentina, Brazil and Venezuela. By the end of 1989, two years after repatriating from Europe, I was offered a position in Brazil, to work with our distributor and help increase our business in that country. I saw the position as a lateral move at best and not appealing at all, as it required a family move to the capital Sao Paulo. I was in no mood to contemplate such move, not only because of family reasons, but also because of the reputation of that city, where foreigners were in a constant state of danger, with robberies, kidnappings and other criminal acts. It was not the best time to move to Brazil and I refused to do so. In retrospect, I made the right decision from a family viewpoint, but it eventually cost me my career at Nortel.

Also, by mid-1989 Canada like other western countries entered one of the longest and deepest global recessions in memory. Investments in high-tech and telecom equipment were reduced to the bone, thereby causing a financial crisis for many companies, NT included. To make things worse, our rate of growth in the last few years had been so high that the company became somewhat blasé and failed to foresee the downturn. As a result, it found itself overstretched with excessive capital investments in new and costly plant facilities and human resources. That situation created a heavy debt level and played havoc with the balance sheet, as sales failed to materialize to overly aggressive budget levels.

Consequently, NT incurred several consecutive quarters of operating losses and the stock plunged, at which point Paul Stern, the cocky and narcissistic CEO, was fired for incompetence. In those uncertain times in world markets many telecom manufacturing companies found it difficult to survive and a few of them merged or were liquidated. Among such casualties, Western Electric, a giant in those days, became Lucent and was eventually taken over by Alcatel, which was later acquired by Nokia. Others, including ITT, Thomson CSF, Philips Networks, Siemens Networks, Italtel, Teleglobe, Mitel and other smaller companies ceased to exist.

NT, after the dismissal of its CEO, did not seem to have the wherewithal to recover and was therefore viewed as limping to its eventual demise, which proved wrong at the time, but right ten years later.

Bell Canada in the meantime had reorganized into a holding company known as BCE (Bell Canada Enterprises), which owned Bell Canada, Bell Canada International and Telesat, and was also majority shareholder of NTL. BCE, led by Raymond Cyr (the same who joined Ben and me in North Africa), took drastic action on NT and appointed a new CEO, Jean Monty, to lead the company back to growth and profitability. Jean was the former President of Bell Canada, a young wizard in his mid forties. He wasted no time in cutting costs and in reducing the bloated management personnel. He also offered generous financial packages to anyone willing to resign or take early retirement.

Many employees accepted the package and left the company. Among them were three former colleagues of mine from London. At 48 I didn't feel old enough for such package and did not take it at first. I continued to work for CALA but a combination of financial tightening and sale stagnation gave me a sense of redundancy. I was then told by some colleagues in similar predicament that it was time for a change. I was in fact due to start my second career in life. Climbing up the executive ladder in three different corporations was considered to be average in those days. So

I looked for opportunities in other high-tech companies with international operations. Unfortunately the economy was in recession in the western world at the time and not much was available at my management level.

However, there were several good opportunities for people with my experience in heading a new start-up company. A lot of money could be made with the right idea and the right people, so I contacted a headhunter and started looking around. In June 1990 I found what I was looking for and talked with Emile to see if the NT package was still available. It was, so I took it.

Immediately thereafter, I negotiated the terms and accepted a job as President of IPS (Image Processing Systems Inc.) located in Markham, Ontario. IPS - a five-people operation - had been in business for three years, working on a new technology that blew me away for the potential it had in future applications. I joined as a third equal partner and agreed to work for six months without pay as part of my investment in the company. I also agreed to provide the company with a short-term loan, much like a line of credit, at going interest rates plus a premium of four percent.

I then left NT with a lot of misgivings and many 'what ifs'. In retrospect it has been my worst decision, not only because I refused the job in Brazil, but also because I was convinced that NT would not survive. That notion turned out to be the worst mistake I ever made in my entire life. But then again, I was about to get into an exciting new career as the President of a promising high-tech start-up. I was therefore not worried about a pension, as I had no intention of ever 'retiring' from a company that I owned a third of. I thought I could go on earning a comfortable living for the rest of my life.

With those ideas in mind and fearing the worst for the future of NT I liquidated and cashed in all of my accrued pension, money that I quickly invested in high-tech securities, convinced that it would eventually grow big time as the high-tech market recovered. As it happened, though, my overall investment did well through the nineties, reaching the two-million-dollar mark in year 1999, but it crashed out badly during the dotcom debacle in the early part of the new millennium. Thus, a pension plan that would have given me well over $5,000/month of income in 2006, at age 65, turned out to be a near total loss in 2002.

Hallelujah!

**

PART TWO

*

IMAGE PROCESSING SYSTEMS

*

A humbling lesson in managing
high-tech start-ups

Chapter Nine

Image Processing Systems

IPS was a small company founded in 1987 by Eric Buckley and Todd Richardson. It ventured into high-tech business by tackling a burgeoning new technology – the fast growing high-speed, high-resolution graphics. It had developed proprietary technology that enabled a faster and better way to process graphic information and thereby quickly interpret in great details a digital image. The applications for such technology were numerous and very exciting.

One of the first such applications the company was working on was a method to visualize CRT screens (used in TVs and Monitors) and calibrate their geometric scanning and focal needs. The calibration was at the time done manually and proved costly and time-consuming. The IPS system enabled a generic operator (not an expert) to do such calibration much faster and better, without requiring expert technicians to do so. The business case was therefore made and provisionally sold, subject to performance verification and approval, to a Philips manufacturing unit in Toronto, who agreed to advance some funds for the project.

A second application was for the poultry industry. It was a system designed to scan deboned chickens on a conveyor belt to identify pieces of bone that got left behind. The way it was done at the time was to have visual inspectors check visually each individual deboned chicken before sending to packaging -- a labor-intensive and costly process. Here too the business case was solid and raised interest in several food processing companies, subject to a working demonstration. Other applications were also possible but each one required long and expensive research periods to develop persuasive business cases.

Todd was a born entrepreneur, chatty and outgoing, and the one who started it all. Eric was an electronics engineer with superior and creative technical abilities, but kept to himself and tended to be very short-tempered. Todd was a had-working optimist (he had to be in that business) but also devious (a necessary trait for entrepreneurs), unrealistic and less than truthful. In my days at Nortel I had learned to abide by a most important tenet that

I had etched on a brass plate hanging prominently on a wall in my office.

It said: "D*o what you say you will do, or don't say it*". It was a more explicit way of saying: "w*alk the talk*" and I made sure all of my staff understood it and adopted it as their tenet as well. But in the case of Todd, abiding by that tenet was a no-no. He was a true entrepreneur, and as such he took high risks in everything he did, including predicting the impossible and spinning reality into fiction or vice-versa, just to 'sell' his ideas. He was very good at it and managed to get the company going by attracting modest investments, as convertible debentures, from a few friends and family members.

When I first talked to him he told me that as a former salesman for a computer company he knew that high-resolution graphic boards were in high demand and that the technology was growing fast. So he decided to get into it but needed a young and ambitious electronic engineer to help him out. So he looked for and found Eric, a highly recommended engineering graduate with Masters and top honors from the University of Waterloo.

"Eric was the best electronics engineer I had ever met," Todd told me. "He was an independent soul, a genius really, and he was

*reluctant to work for anybody, which was
exactly what I was looking for."*

In fact, Eric proved to be Todd's ideal
partner, willing to make short-term sacrifices
for long-term gains. The two of them hit it off
immediately and agreed that Todd would take
care of all administrative and selling activities,
while Eric would concentrate on designing the
best high-res boards ever created. They were a
matched business pair but lacked management
skills and financial experience.

They survived for nearly three years
using small investments from relatives and
friends and having their wives be the bread
winners. But that situation was untenable in the
long run, as Eric needed more and more capital
to purchase expensive tools and solid state
components to experiment with, while Todd
needed money to travel and meet potential
customers. As well, those high-res boards
required a considerable amount of firmware
development, a skill that Eric did not have. It
therefore got to the point where they had to
hire a software expert and, along with him, also
a   secretary/receptionist   to   look   after
administrative   tasks.   Thus   the   overhead
quickly exceeded their meager income (mostly
from Philips and from small testing contracts
Todd managed to get from his former
employer), and could no longer be sustained.
They stopped paying for rent, hydro, telephone

service and salaries and got close to the point of having to file for protection.

Todd's desperate efforts in trying to get additional investments didn't lead anywhere, neither from private investors nor from government agencies, even though the company would have qualified for some assistance programs. Todd's problem was both poor timing due to economic recession and, above all, an inadequate business plan. In the meantime his personal reputation suffered as he kept promising what he could not deliver. The bank manager too became nervous and threatened to foreclose an overdrawn credit line. As to Eric, he stayed out of all money matters and never intervened, except to say at one point that they needed help.

Much to Todd's hesitation he eventually had to accept the fact that they could not survive on their own and set out to find an experienced business partner to lend credibility to the company, help raise funds and set the stage for future growth. This is when they advertised for someone like me and had three serious candidates willing to join. I was eventually selected because, in their words, "as a former Nortel executive I would add credibility to IPS, and also because I looked trustworthy."

In retrospect their choice was more likely made on the basis that I came across as the more naive in entrepreneurial matters and more easily manipulated. Be it as it may I was hooked. I was told that they were well advanced and had already conducted joint testing of their CRT calibrating system with Philips. I requested a meeting with Philips and was satisfied that they were telling me the truth. I was also told that they were on the verge of signing another multimillion dollar contract with General Foods on chicken bone detection systems, but I could not get any confirmation except for a few pieces of correspondence showing interest. I had a good look at their tax filing and did not see anything untoward, other than very little income and a lot of unused tax credits.

To complete my personal due diligence I asked for a copy of their so-called business plan and received a 50-page document replete with big numbers and optimism but with little or no market research and no financial analysis. I was impressed at how enthusiastic it all sounded and decided that I could clean it up and corroborate it with factual data and a solid financial package to add credibility. I was convinced by then that IPS had an edge over competing start-up companies trying to build a better mousetrap, as it were. I saw it as an opportunity for fast growth and for leaving my own stamp on what could have qualified for an

IPO within 3-5 years, or for an outright acquisition by a big company.

However, my lack of experience with venture capital made me overlook the fact that in a period of deep recession venture capital is unavailable for any high-risk company, especially for start-ups. As well, used as I was to work within a large corporation with experts in every facet of business available for assistance and advice, I could not anticipate a situation where I had to play multiple roles entirely on my own.

However, having been pumped up with optimism - a contagious phenomenon with people like Todd - I decided to go for it and joined them as President in July 1990, on two conditions. First: I agreed to make available immediately a short-term personal loan in three tranches of $50,000 each over three months, at 13% rate of interest (at the time the bank charged 9% to their best customers, but I insisted on getting a premium to reflect the risk I was taking). The loan was repayable in full upon securing sufficient capital investments from other sources. Second: I agreed to contribute six months of my time in exchange for a third of all outstanding common shares, thereby making me a third equal partner. The share part was the sticky point that made the deal fall through on two occasions, as they insisted on a lower portion. We eventually agreed to be equal partners, signed the deal, changed the Shareholders Agreement and had it duly notarized and registered.

I quickly rewrote the business plan and set out to contacts various VCs with a compelling set of slides for a dog-and-pony show, and that's when reality hit me like a sledge hammer. Most VCs did not even bother to answer my inquiries and a few months after several fruitless attempts I gave up. I then joined Todd in seeking new contracts that would provide quick cash advances, but even though there was keen interest in what we were proposing, neither General Foods nor others materialized quickly enough. Time was not on our side, but Todd continued to be his usual optimistic self, while I began to waver and lose hope. The company had already received seed money from a couple of early 'angels' and was not seen as qualified for more seed money. What was needed was a 'mezzanine' kind of financing to the tune of at least a million dollar, but at that level there was nothing available, neither in Canada nor in the USA. In 1990-91 we lived through a deep recessionary period in Canada that dried up all VC investment funds.

In that predicament our only salvation was to seek help from the government. Reluctantly, hat in hand, I approached the Ontario Development Corporation for a $200,000 investment loan, in the form of a convertible debenture. I solicited meetings and talked to several key officials until one of them took me seriously and told me that the only way they could help was for me to show that we had a substantial and verifiable purchase order from a serious customer. I knew that I could not provide any such order any time soon and I felt demoralized. As I prepared to leave his office he must have felt sorry for me and whispered a friendly piece of advice. He told me with a wink and a smile that he would accept just a letter of intent to get the ball rolling. I felt belittled, mortified and utterly incapable of playing the part of the enthusiastic entrepreneur. As a former executive of a major multinational I was not used to that kind of humiliation, especially when coming from a civil servant of modest standing, and I was not going to take it any longer. I still had a lot of pride and a sense of dignity in me.

I walked out of the ODC fuming and fully intentioned to put a stop to that charade. I struggled with being the manager, the accountant, the marketer and the beggar all wrapped into one, and decided that that life was not for me. I needed to have a solid team of people working for me and with me, just as I did at Nortel. I was a corporate animal, not a struggling entrepreneur. One cannot grow a start-up to stardom without money, no matter how ingenious and hard-working its founders are. As soon as I got back to my office I updated my CV and sent it to a couple of headhunters. I was determined to take any reasonable job offer from a large corporation, anywhere, but I was also determined not to leave IPS in the lurch. I wanted to leave them with some form of security while looking for a better person to run the show. I therefore renewed my effort with a computer distributor who expressed interest in our high-res boards.

The company was owned and run by an Indian family, with father and daughter as the principals. They were reasonably well known in Toronto and had a decent business in distributing computer components for several companies from Asia. I knew I could talk business with them in a language they surely understood (my business experience in Libya came to mind at that junction). I invited both father and daughter to lunch one day and told them in very specific terms that if they were able to help me I would help them at the first opportunity.

I told them I needed a purchase order for at least $2 million worth of high-res boards, deliverable within a two-year period. They looked at me with a strange smile at first but soon warmed up to the idea and understood why I was asking for the order. They told me that they were interested in an exclusive global distributorship, provided the price was right and the boards performed reliably to spec.   I told them we could work it out along those lines and agreed to meet again for the details.

As the reluctant entrepreneur I had become, I knew that they would probably renege by using any of the caveats embedded in the contract if they couldn't sell the boards fast enough. Consequently, I was not bothered by strict quality and performance conditions, and a low price commitment. I needed the contract to qualify for the ODC cash infusion. Finally, in the early spring of 1991, some nine months after joining IPS and after being educated on the ways of start-ups and venture capital, we signed a $2 million purchase order. The order was full of ifs and buts and was probably not worth the paper it was written on, but it was good enough to be used as proof that we were getting somewhere.

With that contract in hand I returned to the ODC and persuaded them to open a file on us and get going with their usually lengthy and punctilious process of due diligence. At that point I informed my Indian friends to play along and confirm the contract to the inevitable inquiries by ODC. A month later, after completing their due diligence, ODC granted IPS a $200,000 investment. We all celebrated with a sigh of relief. IPS was now safe for at least another year, the time needed to complete the design of high-res boards.

A couple of weeks after closing the deal with ODC I received a call from my head hunter advising that Spar Aerospace was looking for someone with my experience. I jumped on it, in spite of the renewed confidence in IPS future. In retrospect I should have stayed at IPS and continue to struggle through it, but I decided I was not made for that life of constant begging and belt-tightening in a never ending effort to make ends meet. I owed it to my family to go back to an enjoyable lifestyle, with vacation time and some free spending on little pleasures.

We had a condo in Italy with a Jaguar gathering dust in the garage that we had not used since our departure from Rome in 1987. Uncertain times at Nortel and my adventure at IPS had made it impossible to return to Italy for four years. I could not contemplate a few more years of continuing financial restrictions and uncertainty. Also, I was not used to playing so many roles and wearing so many hats as I was doing at IPS, and the thought of joining a large corporation appealed to me.

The job opening at Spar was for a senior director to run a business unit in Montreal. The unit specialized in ground-based satellite communication systems, which fit well with my telecom background. Also, it was organized as a small division, with full P&L responsibilities, which is what I wanted. The only drawback from my point of view was that the position reported to both a small American subsidiary located in California and the much larger satellite division located in Montreal.

My first interview was with Sherin Kamal, the President of the American subsidiary, and my second interview was with Ken Perry, Kamal's boss and also my future boss. I obviously did very well because a couple of weeks thereafter I received an offer of employment. I flew back to Montreal to negotiate the details and returned home with a firm offer in hand. I was given one week to decide whether to accept it and move the family to Montreal.

A couple of days later I invited both Todd and Eric to lunch and informed them of my decision. I told them that with the $200,000 infusion from ODC they were okay. They had good credit from suppliers and were financially safe for well over a year, by which time they would be able to find someone else better suited than I was to run the company. In the meantime I would continue to help on a part time basis and agreed to sell all my shares to the newcomer, provided my outstanding loan was fully repaid with interest. I explained that I had learned a lot at IPS and discovered that I did not have it in me to live the uncertain life of a struggling entrepreneur. I also stressed the point that I did not abandon ship before securing its future and that when it's all said and done they would be better off without me.

They didn't like it and tried to persuade me to stay, stressing that things were getting better and better, and that sooner or later the recessionary period we lived through would end, and that VCs would be back on the prowl, looking for promising small companies to invest in. They pointed out that with my management experience and background I would make IPS more credible to future investors than anyone else coming from the start-up world. At one point I was tempted to go along with their optimism and decline the offer from Spar, but decided to talk with the family before a final decision.

As I revealed the new development to my wife and children, I could see that they were not happy with moving to Montreal. At the time we had Christian and Marc in university in Waterloo, just an hour away from home, and Robert in high school near home. Moving to Montreal, a French-speaking province, implied potential social integration difficulties for Mary and Robert, but it was also an opportunity for acquiring new cultural skills. It also meant that, given the distance, Christian and Marc would not be able to come home on weekends.

As well, upon our return from Europe in 1987 I had purchased a hobby farm with 50 acres of land previously used as a tobacco farm. It was barely 70 Kms from home, and had a huge barn with farming tools, including a functional tractor, two dilapidated kilns and a small cottage. We used it on most weekends all year, including for cross-country skiing in winter, but after four years the novelty wore off, and the enthusiasm of spending so much time there waned as the boys became teenagers and developed other interests. I did not therefore think that moving far away from the farm was a problem.

The most important consideration was a financial one. The senior management position I was offered appealed to me too much to refuse. I knew I could not continue to risk, beg and pray at IPS, and I knew I would be much happier in a financially secure corporate setting. With those thoughts in mind I decided to accept the offer and move the family to the town of Hudson, a suburb of Montreal, fifteen-minute drive from my new office at Spar.

The lesson I learned from IPS is that not everybody is cut out to be an entrepreneur, especially when reeling from a cushy executive position in a major corporation. It's not just the financial stress, but also the humiliation, the hat-in-hand situations, the begging, the rejections from Venture Capitalists and the uncertainties. Entrepreneurs are a special breed of people, especially when they start from zero, without financial support from family and friends. They are dreamers, determined, cheeky, uninhibited, optimistic, patient and willing to rough it out for as long as necessary. I have never been that kind of person nor did I want to even try to be, no matter what the long-term rewards may be.

So I left IPS and moved to Montreal to start a third career. A few months later Todd and Eric managed to find another entrepreneur and shortly thereafter I sold all my shares to him at a decent profit. Three years later the company was sold to an American concern. I have never heard back from either Todd or Eric, but I know that they walked away from IPS with a decent financial reward for their hard work.

***

PART THREE

*

SPAR AEROSPACE

The cultural drawbacks of a medium-sized Corporation used to dealing with government contracts on a cost-plus basis.

Chapter Ten

Spar Aerospace

I moved to Montreal alone in July 1991 to start working at the Spar plant located in Ste Anne de Bellevue, a suburb of west-end Montreal. I left the family in Woodbridge and rented a furnished apartment in the West Island, paid for by the company. It was a necessary move to give us time to sell our house in Woodbridge and scour the Montreal suburbs for a location and a house suited to our needs. Unfortunately the Canadian economy was still in recession and selling a 4300 sqft house in Woodbridge proved very difficult. As a result I extended the rental of the apartment for an entire year and commuted weekly, by car, 550 Kms each way.

In the meantime the real estate market tumbled across Canada, especially in the Toronto area, known to be overvalued. Our house, initially valued at $550,000, had to be reduced three times and eventually sold for $380,000, but was guaranteed by the company at $430,000. Of all the houses we saw in the west suburbs we eventually settled for a large Georgian brick house in Hudson, just off the island of Montreal, fifteen minutes drive from Spar. The market value of the house suffered an identical drop as our Woodbridge one, down to $380,000 from an initial asking price of $550,000.

The house, built in 1988, was a distress sale, due to financial problems and a divorce of the original owners, and had yet to be finished. There was no landscaping, no back terrace and many parts of the interior were left undone. By the time we landscaped it and finished the interior, the house ended up costing me exactly what I had received from the guaranteed sale of Woodbridge, with no gains and no losses. We moved there in October, 1992.

Spar Aerospace was the largest Canadian designer and manufacturer of space-based technologies, including satellite payloads and space robotics. It had revenues of some $600 million and employed well over 4000 people, mostly technical staff. Coming from Nortel, Spar was relatively small but it was the largest in space technologies and one of the better known around the world, having pioneered the design and manufacturing of the first Canadian telecom satellite in orbit.

The company was organized into two basic businesses – the space systems (SSD) and space robotics (SRD), each managed by a so-called 'president'. A third business, dealing with helicopter maintenance, was self-supportive and unrelated to space. Within SSD a smaller division was created, dealing with ground-based satellite telecom systems consisting of large earth stations with antenna dishes exceeding 10 feet in diameter. This division - referred to as GSD (Ground Systems Division) - was in financial trouble and was slated to either close down or find someone to lead it back to profitability. Senior management decided for the latter solution and that's where I came in.

I took over GSD in August 1991 and, after a lot of changes, not just in personnel but also and primarily in the prevailing management culture, I turned it around and made it the most profitable Spar division in less than three years. The management culture I found at Spar was one that grew out of government contracts, mostly done on a cost-plus basis, and therefore cost-driven and free of financial risks, but also unlikely to grow.

GSD was being run the same way, in spite of the fact that they were competing internationally with private companies, not government institutions. Their bids, submitted in answer to international tender calls, were priced by adding all their costs (usually inflated) plus a profit fee. There was little or no knowledge of what competitive forces were at play and what price level they were expected to compete with. As a result most of their bids were either priced too high or too low, thereby missing potentially lucrative contracts or losing money on the ones they won.

I dismantled the existing cost-plus bidding culture and introduced the market-driven approach I had practiced so successfully at NT. The new approach proved useful in three ways: 1) it enabled selective bidding, with sufficient market intelligence; 2) it set prices to competitive market levels, knowing competing forces; 3) it ensured that all costs were calculated to the bone, without the usual 'fat' added by section managers.

To be more specific:

1) No bidding activities were undertaken on any tender call for which there was no readily available market intelligence. This eliminated a lot of wasteful efforts in bidding on projects that we could not win, and it identified areas where we needed to acquire more information.

2) Prices were set to meet or beat market expectations. By knowing what similar projects were sold at, by whom, to whom, where and when, a composite of available market data was thus analysed and extrapolated to come up with the best possible pricing strategy. In all cases the objective was to aim for profitability, or for gain in market share, or

for positioning the company for future opportunities in the same market sector.

3) All costs were analysed in minute details, by negotiating better deals with suppliers and by fine tuning engineering and other manpower requirements. The previous practice of adding 'fat' to all cost elements (e.g. material, engineering, installation, training, warranties and transportation) just to be on the safe side, was thus eliminated, in favour of an overall contingency amount to cover all unforeseen cost overruns.

The result of this change was that each functional manager had to make do with the 'real' cost in their individual budget, not the inflated one they were used to. That way they did not have the liberty to overspend just because the money was 'in the budget'. All cost overruns, if any, had to be fully justified by each functional manager and taken into consideration for future jobs. In most cases the contingency amounts proved to be partly or totally unnecessary and flowed directly to the bottom line.

In the third year the division became the most profitable ever at SPAR, but I did not see a long-term future for our product line based solely on large earth stations. In fact, to ensure GSD long term viability it was necessary to get on board of a burgeoning new technology, known as VSAT (Very Small

Aperture Terminal). Such technology made it possible to make much smaller and more cost effective earth stations, capable of performing like a large one at a fraction of the cost. The technology was not yet fully developed but a number of companies were at an advanced stage and had already installed trial runs with promising results.

Spar anticipated this turn of event and, a few years earlier, acquired small high-tech company in Santa Maria (California) that was seen as having the ability to develop state-of-the-art VSAT technology. The acquisition was meant to eventually expand the GSD satcom purview and diversify its product line. These systems operated at very high frequency bands (Ka & Ku) using small dish antennas (as small as one foot in diameter), and could be installed just about anywhere.

However, SM (Santa Maria division) proved to be a money loser and a drain to Spar. It had a total staff of about 30 employees and was run by Sherin Kamal, a well spoken young man with a PhD in engineering and dual Canadian-Egyptian nationality. The company relied on sales of a first generation of VSAT stations to keep afloat, while focusing its R&D efforts on a new generation, designed to be slimmer, cheaper, more reliable and less costly than competitive systems. However, the lack of visible progress in the development work of the new VSAT put in question its eventual success within acceptable time and cost targets. As a result, it was felt that SM alone could not deliver the VSAT product we were banking on to ensure the survivability of GSD.

A search was therefore undertaken to find the missing pieces and resulted in the acquisition of another small high-tech company -- Comstream (CS), based in San Diego, California. CS was run by Mel Gaffner, a venture capitalist that provided initial seed money and helped raise subsequent cash infusions to eventually grow the company in the electronics component business. It did well for a few years, reaching sales close to $20 million, with some 100 employees, but suffered badly when its product line aged and lost market share to Asian companies.

To revive its fortunes, CS parlayed its technology into telecom subsystems and then jumped onto the VSAT bandwagon by betting all of its R&D efforts on it. This is what caused its financial difficulties, as development costs and timeline had been grossly underestimated.

At the time of its acquisition, however, CS was deemed to be synergistic with SM and close to completing a very competitive VSAT terminal. The two companies, when merged, would have complemented GSD in both product line and skill set, especially in manufacturing and R&D. Consequently, I was a strong supporter of the CS acquisition for I saw in it the possibility of turning both SM and CS as a technology and production base, capable of providing GSD with cost-competitive products needed to ensure its long term growth.

The fact that they were both struggling to survive was therefore a non issue from my point of view, because as cost centers they would not have to worry about profitability. In the meantime the success of GSD in Montreal made it a cash-rich division capable of financing the acquisition, and it was therefore thought that merging the three groups together under GSD management would result in a competitive state-of-the-art VSAT company well positioned to capture a significant share of the available market worldwide. The plan made sense on paper but did not consider competing personalities wanting to have control of the new group.

In fact, the efforts to build the GSD business by absorbing the two American acquisitions and streamlining their product lines met with resistance from their two presidents, Kamal and Gaffner. They had a different plan in mind. They wanted to consolidate the entire operation, including GSD, as a profit center under the CS banner, in St Diego, with its own CEO, operating as a Spar subsidiary. Their plan was diametrically opposite to mine, for it implied turning GSD into a cost center, thereby depriving it of its front-end control, such as setting priorities, selecting target markets, deciding on pricing and other bidding conditions. As a cost center GSD would have had to rely on outsiders for its sales, marketing, business development and budgeting activities.

They knew that I would never go along with such a plan, simply because GSD would not survive as a cost center. In the absence of meaningful manufacturing facilities and advanced R&D labs (a strength for CS & SM), GSD relied almost entirely on its front end, i.e. sales, marketing, business development, product planning, customer support, training, administration, project management. Without the front end it would have been like driving a car without engine and steering wheel.

As a result, they deliberately avoided discussing the details of the plan with me. Instead, they proposed it directly to Bill Fitzgerald (the head of SSD and our common boss) who agreed to keep me out of the loop until the plan was duly fleshed out. I was puzzled by that attitude, considering that I was the only one to deliver a profitable operation in the group. My guess (just a guess) is that as a proud American citizen (with Republican convictions) working in Canada, Fitzgerald wished to go back to the US and probably saw the creation of a strong group as a prosperous American business he would one day lead as its President.

In the meantime Gaffner and Kamal were positioning themselves to be the next President of the new group. Their proposal, which was in effect a 'reverse takeover' by Comstream, was therefore inspired by personal ambition, not by business common sense. Fitzgerald sided with Gaffner and Kamal and preferred the all-American solution. The merger of the three groups - Comstream, Santa Maria and GSD - was not the issue. We all agreed that as a single organization under one management, the group would benefit from economies of scale and significant synergies, but the vision as to how it should be run pitted the American solution, favoured by Gaffner, Kamal and Fitzgerald, against the Canadian solution, favoured by me. I was clearly a minority and lost out.

Fitzgerald proceeded to present the rudiments of their plan to the CEO (John McNaughton) and the Board, arguing that the new and stronger Comstream would make a significant presence in the US market and thereby improve its business prospects. In the ensuing negotiations to formalize and implement the merger, I argued strenuously against it, pointing out three pitfalls.

The first was the fact that, as an advanced country, the USA had no need and no use for VSAT technology. The argument that a strong presence in the USA would improve its business prospects was therefore flawed.

Secondly, the VSAT technology was developed to address emerging markets in Asia, South America and Africa by providing quick and inexpensive telecom networks anywhere. It was a well known fact that those markets were better served from Canada not from the US. Americans were too often seen in those countries as cocky, manipulative, condescending and good only for big-ticket military materiel, not for commercial products. That reality had already been proven by my experience in the Middle East and Africa.

The third pitfall was that the existing American management was not used to selling internationally and had no expertise in dealing with developing countries, whether at government or at private business level. The use of experienced resources from Canada was not under consideration, nor was the hiring of new resources from other companies, given the prohibitive costs involved.

Finally I argued that GSD had no chance to survive as a cost center and that the destiny of a highly qualified and loyal team of some 40 employees would have to be laid off.

For all the above reasons I argued that the proposed merger would only make sense under the management of the cash-rich and market-savvy GSD, with SM & CS as cost centres, given their combined skills in R&D and their production facilities. After all, that was the reason why they were acquired in the first place. But that rationalization was conveniently described as unnecessary 'turf war' by both Kamal and Gaffner who continued to argue for a complete Comstream takeover.

As well, the desire to build strength in the US team was too appealing to Fitzgerald, regardless of the risks involved. So the merger was eventually approved to proceed along the Gaffner-Kamal-Fitzgerald line, and I was sidelined by conveniently 'promoting' me to a corporate job as VP Business Development, still reporting to Fitzgerald.

This situation gave way to a self-destructive power struggle which, with me out of the loop, involved Gaffner, Kamal and Fitzgerald. Each of these gentlemen wanted to be the new President and each embarked on a less-than-ethical campaign against the other two to gain the upper hand.

Gaffner was the most vitriolic, especially against Fitzgerald, by labelling him as an ineffective megalomaniac with a big mouth, little substance and no vision. Kamal was labelled as too technical, given his engineering PhD, with insufficient management experience and afflicted by a narcissistic attitude that did not sit well with his staff. Gaffner was dismissed by both Kamal and Fitzgerald as a non-technical venture capitalist with no experience in major corporations and no understanding of the satellite or telecom markets.

Adding insult to injury, Fitzgerald hired a business consultant to study the situation and advise on what to do. The marching orders, however, were not to suggest which group should be prime but, rather, who was best suited to the job, it being understood that the three groups would be merged under the CS leadership.

The end result was that none of them got the job. Instead, a non-descript and clueless guy by the name of Ron Derry, a manufacturing VP already working at CS, with no P&L management experience and no international exposure, was chosen as a compromise and was promoted to the job. Kamal and Fitzgerald did not survive and were both laid off within a few months of the merger. Gaffner, as the weasel and wily Jewish moneyman he was, managed to get a long term consulting contract with Spar, reporting directly to Cliff Mackay, the corporate

Executive VP, who took over from Fitzgerald and became my boss.

Comstream's new management under Ron Derry, as predicted, showed its incompetence and continued to operate at increasing losses, while GSD (as expected) was soon liquidated. Three years later Comstream was sold out piecemeal at a heavy loss to Spar.

The foregoing sequence of events is an eye-opener and serves as a lesson for any corporation in any business sector planning mergers and acquisitions. The lesson is that no one with self-serving purposes should be in charge of deciding the merits of any potential merger or acquisition. The business case and the depth of research into the merits of the merger or acquisition should be entrusted to arms-length experts without pre-conditions, not to existing management with obvious personal benefits at stake.

When it was all done I, as corporate VP of Business Development, and Gaffner as an expensive consultant, both reported to the same man, Cliff Mackay. It had by then become obvious to all those involved in the GSD-Comstream merger saga that Gaffner and I were not the best of friends. He blamed me for his failure to be the CEO of the expanded Comstream, and I blamed him for ruining a perfectly good business model I created at

GSD. In the meantime Cliff, a former civil servant without much business experience, had inherited the entire SSD organization from Fitzgerald and was swamped with a work load he was not familiar with.

As a result I was left spinning my wheels in an undertaking that did not have much corporate support, and Gaffner was left idling in his California mansion, but was still paid for consulting services he never rendered. This situation lasted a couple of months, until a new and potentially huge business opportunity appeared to capture the attention of the CEO and the Board.

That opportunity, known as Sovcanstar, a Joint Venture between Canadian and Russian companies, was seen as manna from heaven and created a major business discontinuity at Spar. I was asked to lead the JV as President of Sovcanstar.

***

PART FOUR

*

SovCanStar

*

Vicious management backstabbing dooms a promising Russian-Canadian Joint Venture

*

Chapter Eleven

Sovcanstar

In the late eighties, General Discoveries (GD) - a consulting company driven by a couple of ambitious Canadian entrepreneurs with experience in the Russian burgeoning energy market - had what appeared to be a bright idea for a new business opportunity. The Soviet Union was undergoing major structural changes as President Gorbachov attempted to implement Glasnost & Perestroika and hinted at opening the doors to western-style business investments. GD's initial idea was to create a satellite-based private telecommunication network to serve the gas-and-oil energy industry spanning a large swath of the Russian territory, reaching deep into the Siberian hinterland. Such network would have made it easier for oil companies and other energy concerns to operate much more efficiently and thereby generate considerable financial benefits as the Soviet Union prepared to compete in a free-market world.

The two entrepreneurs, Mike Clark and Steve Nichols, drew-up a plan and approached Industry Canada to help develop a business case and then seek initial seed money for the project. As the thinking evolved and some estimates were made, it became apparent that the magnitude of the undertaking was not for the faint of heart and required risk-takers with very deep pockets.

A single geo-stationary communication satellite with a maximum operating life of some fifteen years would cost in the neighbourhood of $200M to develop and put into orbit, an investment that could never be recovered from private Soviet companies alone. As well, a single satellite would be unable to cover the eleven time zones of the Soviet territory. The scope of the project was therefore of major proportions. However, they believed that by expanding the addressable market to most of Europe and Asia, and using financial and technical resources from both Canada and Russia, the investment could generate attractive returns.

As a result, with Industry Canada initial seed money and management help, they developed a business case and embarked on a mission to recruit key Canadian and Russian satellite companies for a joint effort to build and operate the network. In theory the project was not only commercially attractive but also politically desirable, as it would have created a technical and commercial joint venture between East and West of colossal magnitude and importance. The potential Soviet-Canadian technical cooperation in the project was viewed by government officials in both countries as a great example of friendly cooperation in the post-cold-war years of detente. The project was therefore relatively easy to sell, politically speaking, and was quickly supported by both governments.

A joint Russian-Canadian team of experts was then appointed and tasked to do a preliminary feasibility study. The results of such study proved positive and tentatively justified the viability of the project. A Joint Venture (JV) of Russian and Canadian shareholding companies operating in the satellite business was therefore put together and incorporated as SovCanStar, or SCS. It should be noted that at the time the Soviet Union had not yet been dismantled, hence the name SovCanStar, rather than RusCanStar.

The JV combined the complementary technologies of reliable delivery rockets from Russia and the high-tech satellite payloads from Canada. After several months of discussion and many uncertain starts, the JV grew to include three Canadian and three Russian partners, fully supported by their respective government. The companies involved were:

For Canada: **ComDev** (a manufacturer of satellite subsystems, as prime contractor), **General Discoveries** (two entrepreneurs, as the original founders) and **CanCom** (a service provider of satellite-based telecom facilities), supported by **Industry Canada,** with the Canadian Space Agency in tow.

For Russia: **NPO-PM** (as prime contractor for the carrier and launchers), **Intersputnik** (as prime commercial resellers and users) and **Informcosmos** (as sales outlet), supported by **RSA** (Russian Space Agency, as the owners of orbital slots and as the technical watchdogs).

The network was conceived to consist of five geo-stationary satellites placed into available Russian orbital slots with tracking stations in Canada and Russia, covering Western and Eastern Europe, as well as all of the Former Soviet Union (FSU) and parts of Asia. The Canadian team was responsible for funding and building the five payloads, estimated at some C$200 million, and all of its own travel and living expenses. The Russian team was responsible for the launch rockets and carrier vehicles (known as buses) and their placement into appropriate orbital slots, along with all of their living and travel expenses.

The deal was thus deemed to be fairly split at 50-50 in terms of equivalent investments.

Having defined the composition and the objective of the JV, overall duties and accountabilities were allocated to each side. The Canadian side was tasked with raising the necessary funds as a top priority, while the Russian side was tasked with securing the engineering expertise and manpower requirements, along with five orbital slots over the FSU territory. Both sides were also tasked with undertaking joint preliminary technical analysis of the interface requirements between the Canadian payloads and the associated Russian launch vehicles.

ComDev, as the larger of the three Canadian companies (approx $100 million in revenues and some 700 employees), took the lead by appointing its CEO (Val O'Donovan) as Chairman of SCS, and a member of its senior staff, Anita Bartley, as a temporary President with overall project and financial management responsibilities. On the Russian side, Michail Reshetnev, a celebrated space scientist in Russia and DG of NPO-PM, appointed his Deputy, Fyodor Klimov, to manage the Russian team. It should be noted that NPO-PM - based in the city of Krasnoyarsk in central Siberia - was by far the largest Russian designer and manufacturer of satellites and launch vehicles, and controlled most launch pads from the Baikonur Cosmodrome, the Russian space centre in Kazakhstan.

At this point the JV was ready to look for additional Canadian partners and/or investors with deep pockets, as stipulated in the Shareholders Agreement. To do so a convincing Business Plan was needed, along with snappy slide presentations tailored to specific audiences. For reasons unknown to me, but probably due to lack of experience, a Business Plan was commissioned to be written by an outside Canadian consultant of modest means, rather than by the appointed Sovcanstar management, and resulted in a poorly researched and poorly written plan that failed to impress potential investors.

In the meantime the Soviet Union had broken up and their activities in space technologies had been heavily curtailed. The newly created Russian Federation under President Yeltsin found itself in dire straights, reeling from the Soviet break-up and unable to provide funds for most of its national needs, including the military and all of their space programs. As a result NPO-PM was struggling with lack of financial support, as many of their professional employees (managers and engineers) were scrambling for alternative employment elsewhere, in or out of Russia.

Sovcanstar was therefore viewed in

Russia as a major project that would have saved and retained many valuable resources at NPO-PM. As a result, its top management was forcefully and aggressively supportive, as was the management of the Russian Space Agency and associated top government officials, all of whom were hoping to receive financial support from the Canadian side to make the Sovcanstar project a reality.

Amidst this political and financial turbulence in Russia, the Canadian team got cold feet and did nothing to help their Russian partners financially. The initial seed money ($100,000) provided by Industry Canada had been used up and Comdev, as the lead partner, was not big enough to be an interim financier. GD and CanCom were much too small and could only afford to contribute their own expenses. As time went by, not much was being accomplished and eventually their initial efforts came to a virtual halt, with one side blaming the other for lack of progress.

A major bone of contention was on orbital slots, belonging to Russia. The Canadian side insisted that such slots be immediately assigned to the exclusive use of Sovcanstar, while the Russian side insisted that they needed to have full financial commitment from the Canadians before assigning such slots. In retrospect the impasse appeared to be a stalling excuse by the Canadians, given their inability to find financial backing, despite written assurances of support by both governments. One of the problems was the unpredictable political climate in Russia, which the Canadian side used as a justification for the difficulty they encountered in raising funds.

To counter that argument the Russians reiterated their commitment to the project at all levels of authority, including from the mighty Yuri Koptev, Director General of the powerful Russian Space Agency, who reported directly to the President of the Russian Federation. But in spite of all assurances, the doubts and the uncertainty persisted in the West and faith in the project began to fade, after nearly three years of trying without success.

The dog-and-pony shows undertaken by the then SCS management team over a period of many months was aimed at various Canadian companies and at several Institutional Investors. But the effort proved wanting in both substance and style, and failed to raise interest. The increasingly acerbic blame-game among shareholders made it clear that the SCS management was not up to the task and failed to come up with a convincing story. The problem was ascribed to a combination of weak management and a convoluted Business Plan lacking clarity and failing to include sufficient marketing and financial information to be convincing. As a result it became obvious that the JV was headed for failure unless a new and well-heeled partner with management and technical know-how was soon brought on board to revitalize the project. There was only one company in Canada with the ability to do so. That company was Spar Aerospace

At that time Spar was the largest Canadian company specialized in the design and manufacturing of highly sophisticated satellite payloads (i.e. the 'brains', also known as 'transponders' of the orbiting satellite), having already provided such payloads for several communication satellites operating around the world. Spar had been approached several times before but always declined to join as a shareholder, as it preferred to stay in the background, committed only to being a contractor for payloads whenever the JV was fully funded and ready to proceed. As a $600 million company, Spar did not have the financial resources to invest in the JV, but did have both the management and technical know-how to build and deliver, along with the Russian partners, a fully functional satellite network.

Faced with an impending collapse of the JV and the loss of potentially enormous benefits that it entailed, Spar decided to join Sovcanstar as a full partner and equal shareholder on condition that it be the leading member of the Canadian side and appoint a new President chosen from its own senior management staff. It also made it clear that its contribution would be strictly in-kind, not monetary, as each partner agreed to look after its own expenses, except for NPO-PM who required some financing for its work on interface design.

The JV was then revised to include Spar Aerospace, along with Comdev, General Discoveries and CanCom, as equal Canadian shareholders, each with 12.5 % of the shares. Following the agreement, Spar proposed my candidature to lead the JV as its President. I was known for my broad-based international experience, and for my proactive and aggressive management style. Soon thereafter a shareholders meeting was called and held in St. Petersburg, Russia, in October 1993 to approve my appointment and agree on a new action plan. In my acceptance speech I promised to write and present to the Board a new, credible and comprehensive Business Plan during our next Board meeting, due to be held in Canada, in mid-January 1994.

The arrival of Spar as a shareholder and the appointment of an experienced and aggressive President were received with enthusiasm by everyone and bode well for the future of the JV. The Russian partners were somewhat relieved that Sovcanstar had been rescued and looked forward to working together with their Canadian counterparts on all technical, logistic and admin work.

It's worth noting that the English-Russian translation and communication job was made considerably easier by Ms. Olga Romanova, an outstanding interpreter from Moscow, with experience in technical terminology. A lot of planning needed to be done on the technical side, as the interface between the 'payload' (or transponder capsules, built by Spar) had to match to millimetric accuracy the 'bus' (or launch vehicle, built by the Russians). In addition, the work schedules between the two technical teams needed to be synchronized and reviewed periodically to ensure a seamless integration.

In writing the new Business Plan I used bona-fide some of the technical considerations, including timing and manufacturing costs, worked out in preliminary form during the pre-Spar years, but the bulk of the new BP consisted of an in depth analysis of available markets and competitive forces at play, including extrapolated growth patterns and financial projections. I presented the new BP as promised to the Board in mid-January 1994, after two months of intensive work right through the Christmas holidays. I consulted various market research publications to size up the marketplace, analyse the competition, estimate service requirements in each of the several markets covered by the network, and combine it all in a convincing story, fully corroborated by factual data and realistic projections. The Board was both impressed with the plan and relieved to see it done in such short time. The business case had therefore been made and all was set to initiate a search for private investors with deep pockets and, if possible, with commercial synergies.

The first few potential investors to be approached in Canada were Teleglobe, BCI (Bell Canada International), and Northern Telecom. These were three successful Canadian telecom companies operating internationally in complementary fields of expertise, and were therefore seen as potentially strong partners.

Teleglobe was a public company controlled by Charles Sirois, a business tycoon who created Teleglobe from zero and built it into a global billion-dollar corporation. As a long distance satellite-based telecom company headquartered in Montreal, Teleglobe was seen as a prime target for partnership, given their heavy use of satellite facilities for world-wide long-distance services. They appeared to be interested at first but, as it turned out, they were more focussed on learning about Sovcanstar plans and those of competing companies than they were in investing anything in the project. All of the meetings held with Teleglobe were pointless and useless one-way information sessions. They were eventually told to get lost.

Bell Canada International (BCI) was part of Bell Enterprises, a family of telecom companies that included, inter alia, Telesat and Bell Canada. BCI made money in providing consulting services on how to run a public telephone company. As such BCI was instrumental in setting up, organizing, running and training the Saudi Arabian telecom network over a period of ten years. Similar contracts were also signed with other companies around the world, mostly government-owned entities.

BCI made an honest effort in trying to understand how they could provide profitable services using Sovcanstar network, but were unable to come up with a sound business case. The main problem was that Sovcanstar had no ground infrastructures and relied on selling its services to established telephone or satellite TV companies around the world. In other words Sovcanstar acted much like a mirror in space, capable of reflecting down to a large footprint on earth whatever was beamed up to it. BCI did not have ground facilities anywhere other than in Canada and could not therefore benefit from Sovcanstar without risky and prohibitive investments.

Northern Telecom (my alma mater) - which by then had been resuscitated from its earlier crisis - had deep pockets but no obvious interest other than being a good corporate citizen. They were approached at my personal insistence, given my special relationship with that company, but was quickly discarded for two reasons: they were not in the satellite communication business and had no useful experience to bring to the table. As well, they were too busy in developing a new generation of digital technology to consider a new venture into space-based communications. They did reserve the right, however, to do so at a more propitious time.

Having given up on those three major Canadian prospects there remained nothing else to do but go after international investors, especially in Europe. A major thrust was made with EBRD (European Bank for Reconstruction and Development), a financial organization based in London, England, and funded by western governments, including Canada. The EBRD was born soon after the collapse of the USSR and was tasked with providing financial assistance to countries of the FSU (Former Soviet Union) to help them develop needed infrastructural projects. Sovcanstar was therefore seen as the perfect project to be financed under EBRD auspices, for it would have provided quick and cheap telecommunication facilities anywhere in the entire FSU territory without major investments on ground networks. With this in mind, I established contacts and set up meetings in London to make a case for the project.

The first meeting with EBRD officials took place in March 1994 in London, England. I presented the business case and officially applied for part of the necessary funding, leaving behind a copy of the business plan and related documentation on the composition of the JV and support by both Russian and Canadian governments. The presentation was very well received and was followed two weeks later by a more in-depth risk analysis, along with the pros and cons for the FSU and Eastern European economies (the EBRD's raison d'être).

I was then invited to make the case at the next Board of Governors meeting in St. Petersburg, Russia, in May 1994. At that meeting I gathered together the top brass of the Russian satellite industry and, together, they made a compelling case in support of Sovcanstar. EBRD officials were convinced and followed up with a letter of interest, followed soon thereafter with a draft Agreement detailing the terms of their participation.

The prospects for a successful financing operation with the EBRD for a large chunk of the required funds were thus quickly materializing and made it easier to go after institutional investors world-wide for the balance. To do so a Financial Advisor of international repute was needed to put together a prospectus and initiate a world-wide search for a group of investors willing to contribute the remaining investment. At EBRD recommendation and after considering other options, I chose Solomon Brothers (SB), based in London, and contacted them soon after the Board of Governors meeting in St. Petersburg. A first meeting in London was quickly followed, at SB request, by a second in Paris, (I was attending a conference in Versailles at the time).

At that meeting, held at the Meridien hotel, four high-ranking officials from Solomon Brothers flew to Paris to meet with me. They presented their plan on how to raise the remaining capital requirements for the project and were enthusiastically prepared to get going, working only on a share of the proceeds thereby making it risk-free to Sovcanstar. I found the proposal attractive and promised to get back to them as soon as I had a chance to discuss it at the next Board meeting.

In the meantime the project was looking more and more real even from a technical viewpoint and gained visibility in the business media, with interviews from business magazines being sought and granted in North America, Europe and Russia. Competing satellite companies from around the world, including Intelsat, Panamsat et al, took notice and watched closely Sovcanstar market moves. An air of optimism was palpable among all shareholders, especially at the technical level, as engineers from both countries worked feverishly to complete their design in time to start construction work. The project became the most important undertaking at both Spar and NPO-PM, as both needed it to remain viable in very difficult financial times.

In tandem with the progress being made on both the financial and the technical fronts, potential users of the network began to knock at the door with requests for quotes and transponder service availability. They were service providers from a number of countries, including China, India, Brazil and Argentina, all heavy users of satellite communication facilities for both Telephony and Television.

A case in point was Chinasat, a new Hong Kong company created by Richard Lee, a well-known Hong Kong billionaire and aggressive businessman. Lee contacted me and explained that Chinasat had immediate need for transponder space required to provide telecom service to emerging sectors of mainland China. Lee was willing to pay five million dollars for the use of a temporary transponder, as a bridge to Sovcanstar, if it could be provided on short notice.

He knew that Russia had space available on one of its existing satellites - a Gorizont series operated by Informcosmos (a Sovcanstar shareholder) - and also knew that it had already been committed to an Indonesian company. Lee believed that with enough cash Informcosmos could be persuaded to reassign such transponder to Chinasat, thereby denying service to a competing company. In a telephone conversation, I discussed the opportunity with Mr. Tsyrlin, the DG of Informcosmos, who agreed that the satellite in question was located in an ideal orbital slot covering a large footprint of mainland China, and still had a few years of service life in it.

Attracted by the conspicuous sum of money being offered, Tsyrlin took an interest in it and requested an urgent meeting with me in Moscow to discuss a possible plan of action. The opportunity for immediate and substantial cash infusion was viewed as a God-sent by the struggling Russian company and was therefore accepted, subject only to devising a reasonable way to justify the reassignment.

The meeting took place as requested but, at Tsyrlin's insistence, it was held during a walk in the Moscow woods, away from indiscrete ears. The plan being proposed was to use SCS as prime for a long-term contract with Chinasat; SCS would then subcontract the transponder from Informcosmos until SCS was up and running. That way Tsyrlin could tell the Indonesians (who had not yet made any payments) that he was forced by his commitment as a shareholder to reassign the transponder to Sovcanstar. I balked at the deviousness of the idea but I was eventually persuaded and I promised to play along.

It should be noted that the satellites operated by Informcosmos were of the small but successful Gorizont series, designed by NPO-PM and placed in inclined orbits years earlier to serve the need of the USSR, mostly military. They were equipped with several full-size transponders and had a few years of service life left, just enough to make do till Sovcanstar was up and running.

As these promising international events took place, and as the credibility of Sovcanstar was no longer in doubt, old and destructive power struggles and turf battles began to re-emerge on the Spar front. To understand the reasons and the ego-driven motivators behind such detrimental doings, I need to quickly summarize what was happening at Spar when I was appointed to lead Sovcanstar.

It was soon after the ill-conceived Comstream merger that the Sovcanstar involvement by Spar materialized, and it was therefore a welcome coincidence to have me available and willing to lead the JV. Unfortunately the power struggle initiated at Comstream between Mel Gaffner and me (the only two survivors of that battle) did not die with my secondment to Sovcanstar. In fact Cliff, who was instrumental in my appointment, also appointed Mel to work as a part-time consultant for Sovcanstar, reporting to him with dotted line accountability to me. Mel was seen as having financial expertise that would have helped me in securing financing for Sovcanstar. I accepted him on my team with some reservations, but decided to set aside previous disagreements and make the best of his skills in the financial arena.

As it happened, however, it became quickly obvious that Mel had no experience and no feel for large projects, and could not contribute meaningfully to any activity undertaken at Sovcanstar. He was good at raising seed money for start-ups, not major capitals for public companies. In spite of a couple of attempts at getting his inputs on financing strategies, I could not and did not use his services, nor did he care much, for he had no desire of reporting to me on any issue. As a result, the previous personal dislike re-emerged between us and, while my objective was to make Sovcanstar a reality as soon as possible, Mel's personal objective was to secure his position in a permanent top management role and moved quietly behind the scenes to replace me as President of Sovcanstar.

To do so he started to build a case against me, by discrediting me behind my back. He used the well known technique of issuing innuendoes and outright lies on my activities, making it look like I had a hidden agenda against Spar. He argued that I did not digest the fact that I was sidelined in the Comstream merger and was seeking revenge by hurting Spar in favour of the other shareholders. Such accusation was not only an outright lie but also viciously slanderous. He managed to persuade a naive Cliff that I could not be trusted, despite the obvious success I was having with re-launching Sovcanstar, and despite the praise I received on numerous occasions by all Board Directors.

Unfortunately I was unaware of Mel's finagling till much later and did therefore nothing to defend myself from unfounded accusations I was not aware of. What kept me going was the strong support I received from two of Cliff's colleagues at corporate: the CFO (Tony Anderson) and the legal counsel (Sheldon Polanski). I was also strongly supported by two top colleagues at SSD, Claude Filiatrault (VP legal) and Phil Quenneville (VP Finance).

At noticing his difficulties in besmirching me, Mel adopted an additional technique. He befriended John Stuart (the VP of sales at SSD, hired months earlier from the UK) and connived with him. In turn, Stuart hired another consultant from the UK specializing in business plans for the satellite industry, and together they proceeded with suggesting that my business plan needed to be upgraded.   Cliff became nervous at that suggestion, worrying that the JV was headed in the wrong direction, and agreed to consider approving (on Sovcanstar behalf) some $150,000 for a new business plan, developed by the UK consultant.

At this point it became clear to me that I was being manipulated and discredited by Gaffner and Stuart, in spite of the considerable progress achieved and the full support of the Board. I also felt my authority diminished by Cliff's notion that he was free to overrule my decision without Board approval.

As the President responsible for the financial health of the JV, I objected to spending that much money for another and unjustified business plan, considering that Solomon Brothers had already accepted to produce their prospectus based my BP. I therefore refused to approve the funding, arguing that a new plan should be considered if and only if the existing one proved flawed or insufficient, which was far from so being at that stage. The case was eventually reviewed by the Board who sided unanimously (except for Cliff) with me. The rift between Mel Gaffner and me had thus become visible to all and was not conducive to a healthy business atmosphere, whereupon I told Cliff I did not wish to have Mel involved in any activity pertaining to Sovcanstar, whether directly or indirectly. This move did not go down well with Cliff who by then had been persuaded by both Mel and John that I had a hidden agenda against Spar.

It's important to understand at this point that my authority as the President of Sovcanstar was somewhat limited by the fact that I was seconded to the job by Spar and was therefore still, technically speaking, on Spar's payroll. In Sovcanstar I was accountable to the Board of Directors, but as a Spar employee I was still accountable to Cliff, who expected me to do Spar's interests ahead of Sovcanstar, a situation that made other shareholders nervous.

In fact, all Board Directors (except Cliff) made it clear to me on the day I was appointed that as President I was to uphold equitably the interest of ALL shareholders, not just one, and that even though I was still on Spar's payroll my salary and expenses were being absorbed in toto by the JV. I agreed to be equitable and to act accordingly, a fact that was quickly viewed by Cliff as being contrary to Spar's interests. By challenging Cliff's decision, I acted as a defender of all shareholders, but Cliff did not see it that way and decided to join Mel and John in their effort to replace me at the earliest opportunity, which is exactly what Mel wanted from day one.

In that corrosive atmosphere Cliff authorized Mel and John to team up with the UK consultant and produce the alternative business plan as previously suggested. Cliff agreed to pay for it through Spar, thereby sidestepping me. In the ensuing few weeks I was warned by my friend Quenneville that Cliff and Mel were plotting against me. In fact, at a Spar operations review that I used to attend regularly, I was not invited. It became clear at this point that I was being isolated from the Spar contingent, even though the other shareholders continued to be fully supportive.

The optimism about the project in the meantime made Cliff propose that Spar increase its share by providing extra financing to the tune of $1.2 million. I did not think it was necessary but could not say no to extra cash infusion and agreed to work with the other shareholders to agree on a fair share distribution. I flew to Moscow in September with Benyon (SCS lawyer) in tow and, after agreeing with the Russian team on the terms and conditions, I drafted a revision to the Agreement (I did so at night in my hotel room).

The following morning Benyon read and approved the legal elements of the draft and gave a copy to Olga for translation into Russian. Back to Canada the draft was submitted to the Canadian team and was approved unanimously. I was praised for the fairness and celerity with which such changes were made. Cliff too expressed his appreciation.

The way in which that important step was implemented should have been an eye-opener for Cliff, as it proved that I had no hidden agenda and represented fairly and effectively the interest of all shareholders, as recognized by everyone else. But that was not to be. I learned later that the reason why Cliff decided to increase Spar's share was to make sure SCS had enough cash available to pay for the UK consultant ($150K!). Also, knowing that the Russian partners would never agree to have Mel replace me, Cliff tasked John and Mel with initiating a surreptitious search for a new President, by engaging a head-hunter in Europe. The game was getting uglier and uglier as Cliff, Mel and John increased the pressure on me.

While these machinations were going on, I called a shareholders meeting in Windsor, England, in August 1994, where I presented the state of affairs at SCS, reviewing all that was accomplished and the activities underway to complete the financing operations. The EBRD case was reviewed in details and so was the Solomon Brothers proposal. The Russian team was visibly pleased and upbeat about the state of the JV and went out of their way in praising me for what was accomplished, but they were unaware of what was happening behind the scenes. They only knew that Cliff was not happy with my refusal to play his game and suspected foul play.

In private talks during breaks, both Reshetnev and Milov, the two most powerful men on the Russian team, assured me of their support and encouraged me to continue my work the same way, by being impartial to ALL shareholders. The same level of support I received from Michael Clark of General Discoveries. With such overwhelming support I felt secure and determined to complete my negotiations with the EBRD and Solomon Brothers.

Following the Windsor meeting Cliff, Mel and John, all three of them in separate memos, informed both the EBRD and Solomon Brothers that Spar no longer supported my Presidency and that they would not continue to finance SCS with me at the helm. They had no authority to do so, but on the strength that Spar was the major stakeholder and the de-facto decision maker on the Canadian side, they were believed. A period of soul-searching ensued, with the Russians continuing to support me and the Canadian side slowly retreating behind Spar. It became difficult for me to continue under the circumstances, as further progress on the financial front came to a halt.

A new shareholders meeting was then called for by the Russians, to be held in Krasnoyarsk, NPO-PM headquarters in central Siberia. The Russian team wanted to make sure once and for all that I was and remained President of SCS and that only a vote by the Board could change that. At that point, Cliff felt they could not win a Board vote and decided on a new strategy.

He informed me that I had no choice but to resign as President of SCS, while remaining VP at Spar, failing which Spar would exit the JV and cause its liquidation. Cliff was probably bluffing, but he did have the support of Spar CEO John MacNaughton who, later, refused to meet with me to clarify the situation. The issue with Spar was centered on the fact that Cliff wanted to charge SCS large amounts of expenses that were never incurred nor ever approved by SCS. He wanted to do so to artificially increase its share of the SCS JV and reinforce Spar's balance sheet. I refused to play that game despite several attempts by Cliff to do so. In the end, I agreed to resign for the benefit of the JV and accepted to stay on at Spar as VP Business Development.

Upon hearing of my resignation, the Russians faxed a long memo asking me to stay and fight it out, but it was too late. In retrospect, had I attended the meeting in Krasnoyarsk, I would have received full support and would have remained President, but in an unfriendly atmosphere at Spar, with questionable chances of success. A few weeks later, with my resignation in hand, Cliff announced the change to the Board. The Russian team did not take the news kindly and demanded that my resignation be rejected, pending a thorough analysis of what was happening at Spar. At this point Cliff exercised Spar's financial power and threatened all other shareholders that unless I was replaced, Spar would no longer continue to finance the JV.

Following my resignation the Russian side, angry at seeing me forced to leave, refused to appoint Mel as my replacement and tasked the Canadian team to look for an outsider. Cliff, having anticipated such request, presented the new candidate (whose name I do not remember) they had headhunted in Europe and called for a vote for his official appointment. He lasted only two months and was fired for incompetence, while costing SCS (hence Spar) a lot of wasted money. Finally, after shying away from another headhunting fiasco, Mel was appointed President

As VP of Business Development at Spar, still reporting to Cliff, I worked on a number of minor cases for strategic alliances with space-based companies, including Hughes Aerospace and Alenia. I also represented Spar on a South American business trip with Prime Minister Jean Chretien, in which I established senior business contacts in Argentina, Brazil, Chile and Paraguay. However, despite my efforts to show an amicable attitude with no rancor, the relationship between me and Cliff did not show signs of improvements.

His reluctance to be on friendlier terms was probably due, at least in part, to the lack of progress in Sovcanstar. Mel, having been appointed President, showed his true colors as a charlatan, always promising what he did not understand and could not deliver. The costly Comstream debacle was still fresh on Cliff's mind and the possibility of facing a similar debacle with Sovcanstar worried him a lot. The stakes were therefore very high and as time passed without breakthroughs, and available cash dwindled, Spar was quickly approaching the day when it would be forced to exit SCS and fight for its own survival.

As I expected, Mel quickly burned all the available cash on unnecessary and expensive consultants, including uncapped personal expenses, and accomplished nothing. A few months thereafter Sovcanstar was dissolved and Spar was left holding the bag with a big financial hole from which it could not recover. A couple of years later Spar was sold out piecemeal and ceased to exist. This is the sad end of a business story torn apart by personal envy, pride, ambition and management incompetence at all levels. In the meantime, I searched for new opportunities and eventually landed a job as President and CEO of Networks Sciences International Communications Inc, a small Montreal-based VSAT company struggling for survival.

As I think back to my role in Spar's final demise, I realize I have been less than understanding of other people's feelings. Had I been more cooperative and, above all, more diplomatic during the negotiations to merge CS, SM and GSD I would have probably changed the course of events, but not necessarily for the better. I have often been able to compromise on different versions of what's right, but I have never been willing to compromise on what I believe to be fundamentally wrong, especially when devious and dishonest methods are used.

I have been accused of having the tendency to be intransigent, often rejecting arguments and solutions that may have some merit, but I have never been accused of being an opportunist and a hypocrite. I have always been honest to a fault in business dealings at all levels, and have always negotiated in good faith -- I should have known better!

Be it as it may, when strong personalities butt heads, it usually ends up in lose-lose outcomes. *C'est la vie!* I am still convinced, however, that had I stayed on as President of SCS I would have been successful in funding it and making it a reality. It would have been a dream-come-true and an example of how to harness the incredible technical synergies available between East and West. Requiem to a dream!

PART FIVE

*

Network Sciences International

*

How a small publicly traded small company is manipulated by venture capitalists

*

Chapter Twelve

NSI Communications

NSI Communications Inc. was a small public company of some 35 people, struggling to survive and in urgent need of capital infusion. In its early existence, the company - which was initially registered as simply NSI Inc - had developed certain subsystems used in satellite communication applications and looked poised for fast growth, which attracted early investments and went public. However, its sales projections never materialized and its product line aged fast and quickly became obsolete. Facing bankruptcy, its inventive management created a parent company, registered as NSI Communication Inc, having control over NSI without assuming potential liabilities. It then proposed the development of a conceptual design for VSAT systems based on a drastically different approach, using state-of-the-art technology and unique solutions for voice and video modulation and transmission techniques. The idea was obviously well presented and well received by the few investors who kept the company afloat.

The VSAT system they had in mind was conceptually designed by two oft-described 'geniuses', one in hardware and the other in software. The hardware one, Ben K (a late fifties Tcheck guy with an advanced degree in engineering), was also the original founder of the company and its long-time President. The software guy, Mike H (much younger than Ben), was a software specialist who worked with Ben from day one and was co-responsible for the overall design.

Ben and Mike believed that their modulation technique would use a much narrower transmission bandwidth and thereby save a bundle on satellite transponder usage. The system was therefore described as having better performance at half the price of competitive systems. A crude bread-board model built to prove its alleged capabilities (hard-wired rather than via satellite link) was demonstrated to potential investors as evidence that there was some meat on the bones and that the conceptual design was credible and doable.

Ben was a colorful character, with some charisma and technically very strong, especially in hardware design. His long-winded technical presentations and inflated sales and profits projections became well known to the investment community over the years and ended up giving Ben a less-than flattering reputation. During his five-plus years as the NSI President, Ben became known as a wizard of technology, but also a bit of a dreamer and a charlatan who promised a lot without delivering much. As well, he proved to have no management skills and no control over financial matters, leaving it all to a technically clueless CFO with a personal agenda.

Mike, on the other hand, was considered a wizard in software design, with a very fast grasp of what needed to be done, but he was also a brash prima-donna, used to work whenever he felt like, with either long day-and-night sessions or with several days of inactivity and absence from the office without justifications. However, in spite of his shortcomings, he became the indispensable man in motion on the VSAT development, for nothing could be accomplished on the software front without his input. As well, in addition to his erratic and insubordinate behavior, he was a disaster in documenting whatever he was doing. The entire software plan and its individual modules were resident solely in his mind. The only notes available were on hard drive (nothing on paper) and were written only for his benefit, without generic explanations. This situation became unmanageable as the system grew more and more complex and resulted in a series of milestone delays that upset a lot of related activities. In Mike's mind, scheduled milestones were meaningless management idiocies not worth worrying about.

Such character flaws were not known to new investors when NSI Communications was created. Some of them were attracted by the idea that two geniuses were about to revolutionize the satcom industry and were therefore worth risking some money on. Among such investors were four individuals, including Ben, who became major shareholders, each with a seat on the Board and a management role in the company.

The most important of these was David Ben D, a smart and qualified Chartered Accountant whose Jewish family (not him) invested, cumulatively, a considerable amount in NSI, thereby becoming a major shareholder. David, as CFO, took control of all admin and financial activities without much supervision from anyone, including Ben. In fact Ben relied entirely on David on financial matters and never questioned anything. Consequently, many transactions, including certain debts, never appeared on the balance sheet. David was also keenly observant of the Jewish faith and on Fridays, come hell or high water, he would take off for Sabbath.

Another gentleman, Mark S, was a former executive of a multinational corporation who chose to invest in NSI with the proviso that he be given a seat on the Board and appointed VP of Marketing. He was close to his retirement age and worked only to keep active while hoping to eventually make some money from his shares. Mark was a well-dressed and well-spoken gentleman, with credible marketing know-how, but no products to sell. He ended up employing his time looking for sales opportunities for a product that did not yet exist, often travelling and generating marketing material for conferences and exhibitions around the world.

Three more major investors were Board members but did not have a direct role in managing the company. One of them was a retired CA who wanted a management role but could not find any; he remained a vociferous Board member demanding results. The other, Steve S, represented a company of venture capitalists with two seats on the Board. They propped up NSI on numerous occasions with emergency cash infusions in exchange for more and more common shares and convertible debentures. Steve's group eventually became the major shareholder, with Steve as the de-facto (but not appointed) Chairman of the company. It was Steve who, in agreement with David, decided that the situation with Ben at the helm was no longer sustainable and that drastic management changes with a new CEO needed to be made fast to avoid bankruptcy.

Ben had lost all credibility and was no longer taken seriously. A pilot network provisionally sold to a company of service providers in Prague (compliments of Ben's connections to his old country) did not perform anywhere near expectations and frequently broke down, requiring constant and expensive babysitting. A similar network sold to a company in China was also malfunctioning and became the object of an impending lawsuit. Based on those initial sales, Ben had managed to hire some 30 technical people, mostly new immigrants from Eastern Europe, and created jobs that did not contribute much to the VSAT development.

By the time Steve and David decided to look for a new CEO, the Board of Directors consisted of six people, including two seats held by Steve's group, plus Ben, David, Mark and a Florida resident who gave Steve power of attorney. As a result, a decision by Steve and David had the necessary four votes out of six to give them full powers to make whatever management changes they deemed necessary. They hired a headhunter who eventually contacted me and set up an appointment.

In my first interview with Steve and David they painted a rosy picture of NSI capabilities and its potential growth in the

VSAT business. I was told of their contract in Prague and China, and of other contracts in the making, including systems in Venezuela and Chile. I was given a copy of their marketing brochures that described in enthusiastic terms the cost-effective performance and the advanced technical elements of the system being developed. They both intimated that with the right leadership the company was poised for big things and that they needed someone to make sure it would happen in timely fashion and within an acceptable budget. I was told that Ben had lost credibility and that, while he was an excellent technical man, he had no organizational or management abilities, which was directly responsible for the precarious situation they were in. I was also assured that the company was on solid financial ground, given the full support of a major group of venture capitalists who would ensure its short-term survival and future growth. I was also told that Ben did not know he was being ousted and that they wished to keep him in the company in a technical capacity, given his knowledge of the development work still in progress.

After a second meeting, which included Mark and a second capitalist from Toronto, I was told that in view of my experience in both large and small companies, and being fully conversant with the VSAT product line and market forces, I would be 'hitting the ground running'. I was therefore informed that they were willing to make me an offer that would meet my salary expectations and would include a considerable number of common shares. A week later, in September 1995, as I was vacationing in France, I received a written offer, faxed to my hotel, requesting a quick reply. I accepted on condition that certain aspects of the offer be negotiated upon my return to Montreal, which is what we did in October. I also agreed to keep Ben on as VP of Technology, to ensure a seamless management transition at the technical level.

A General Shareholders Meeting was then called for in November to approve my appointment and other matters. Ben was told of his demotion in private talks with Steve and David only a few minutes before the meeting. I did not particularly like the deviousness with which it was being done, but there was no obvious alternative for a more ethical solution. As it happened, however, the news didn't seem to bother Ben and in fact it seemed to even please him. He noted that as a major shareholder he would benefit from new blood at the top and was encouraged to learn of my background and experience. He would thus be able to focus entirely on his development work without worrying about admin duties.

At the end of the meeting he shook hands with me and assured me of his cooperation and support. I found his attitude very constructive and, in turn, I assured him that I would do my very best to re-position the company for successful growth.

Having so established the modus operandi, I remained skeptical about some organizational aspects of the deal. What bothered me was that as CEO I was in charge of the destiny of three senior people in my cabinet, all of whom were also Board Directors and major shareholders. In other words I had the power of deciding their individual destiny, but they had the collective power of deciding my destiny. At that juncture, however, I did not lose too much sleep on it and believed that they needed me more than I needed them, and was confident that we would find a way to work well together.

I took over NSI officially in November 1995, but the mess I found the company in - both in terms of organizational structure and on financial matters - did not make me feel in control. Their offices were located in a very old building in the Town of Mount Royal and were an eyesore to behold. The disorder in that place cannot be described and left a very bad taste in my mouth. I set out to interview all employees, asking each one of them what their role was in the company and what relevant experience they had. It took me a solid week to interview everyone and understand what they were doing. I was not impressed.

Some could hardly speak English or French, others seemed to have no relevant experience, and a couple more appeared to be way overqualified for what they were doing. One in particular from the Ukraine claimed to have a PhD in engineering and was an expert in antenna dishes. He was asked to conduct a study on elliptical dishes, something that was totally irrelevant to VSAT development. Another was tasked with developing a power amplifier for high frequency transmission, forgetting that such units were available from several suppliers at reasonable prices. There were other cases disconnected from reality that upset me and gave me a sense of betrayal. At the end of the exercise I could only count seven people contributing meaningfully to the development work, and none of them was helping Mike in software development.

As Christmas approached and the facility closed down for two weeks, I asked for all financial statements and a list of suppliers, creditors and anyone associated with the company, whether as minor shareholder or as consultants. I took the whole package of paperwork home and analyzed it over the Christmas holidays.

The financial books were a mess, but neatly done. Nothing made sense but all was organized professionally. It revealed to me that David, as the wily CFO, had cooked the books in such a way that few people could understand what the real financial situation was. I had been around financial statements from three different points of view, from Nortel to IPS to Spar and I knew very well that what I needed to see was not there.

The balance sheet had big numbers without explanations or corroborating documentation, neither in the assets nor in the liabilities sections. The cash flow analysis did not make any sense and the P&L for yearly or at least quarterly budgets did not exist. The list of creditors did not seem to match the numbers in the balance sheet and the yearly losses did not add up to cumulative numbers shown in the income statement. I was left with the distinct feeling that the company was flat broke. I got back to the office in January with more questions than answers.

In subsequent meetings with both David on financials and Ben on technology I failed to get rational answers. David insisted that the company had been struggling to survive for years and that he had to be creative in structuring financial statements. Ben argued that all employees would eventually prove their worth as the company expanded into other product lines, forgetting that there was no cash available to do so and no plan either.

In mid January I called a meeting with Steve, David and Ben and informed them that, given the messy state the company was in, I was not going to stay, as I had other opportunities in mind. In mid-December, in fact, I received a promising inquiry from a headhunter about a position at Canadian Marconi as VP Marketing, an opportunity that I was very interested in and to which I had not yet responded.

On hearing of my disappointment and my intention to quit, all three of them became very aggressive in persuading me to stay, even agreeing to raise my salary and other benefits to make it more attractive to me. They told me I had carte blanche to make any changes I deemed necessary and that the technology had been developed already to a pretty good stage, as proven in the pilot network operating in Prague. They even showed me a letter of satisfaction from Prague on how much progress had been made and how close they were to completing the development (I later learned that the letter was written as a favor to facilitate investment activities). I told them I would think it over.

The following day Steve contacted me and told me they were ready to raise my remuneration package and support my efforts to raise fresh cash, in excess of $5 million, from institutional investors. All that was needed, he stressed, was my leadership to give investors renewed confidence and a good story. He was very persuasive and I decided to stay. I soon set out to write a new business plan (I had become an expert at it) in which I emphasized the competitive nature of our VSAT technology and the growing available markets worldwide, drawing on my knowledge and experience from my days at Spar.

A few weeks thereafter we were ready to hit the investment community with the traditional 'dog and pony' show, and by the end of March we raised much more than we expected, with 7 million common shares at $1 each in new investments. Unfortunately, the new investments came with the addition of two new Board Directors, on of whom was an Indonesian VC, a friend of Steve's, while the other was a former Canadian Senator, friend of the Indonesian VC. As a result, Steve could count on five votes out of nine and still retain control of the Board.

I did not think much of this new power center at the time and never worried. We celebrated the success and agreed to upgrade the company in more ways than one. I wanted to move to better premises, remove all unnecessary employees and hire a few new talented people to help speed up development work.

First of all we had to clean up the balance sheet and pay overdue salaries, including payroll taxes, along with a number of critically delinquent long-term debts. In so doing, I discovered a few so-called 'consultants' not shown on the list of creditors. Some were owed money without ever submitting an invoice. David explained that those were verbal agreements needed to make the balance sheet look better, and was part of what he described as his 'creative' accounting work. I was therefore asked to sign cheques without any written evidence of services rendered, based solely on David's word.

I chose to trust him and signed, but I also checked with Ben and Mark who confirmed the authenticity of those debts. I was not used to those devious ways and the experience left a bitter taste in my mouth. By the time it was all said and done we had spent over $2 million in paying old debts and had enough money left over for at least a year of operation with a drastically restructured organization.

A couple of months later we moved to new premises in Ville St Laurent and purchased new, inexpensive office furniture, computer equipment and some badly needed test instruments. Ben insisted on having a large 8ft-dish antenna installed on the roof to conduct transmission tests in C-band, something very expensive and not absolutely necessary for VSATs operating in Ku and Ka bands, but helpful.

The antenna was eventually purchased and installed despite my initial disagreement. As I tried to set a budget and milestones I became more and more frustrated at the inability to get any reliable information on development timelines and costs. Ben would tell me whatever I wanted to hear with no rationalization, while Mike told me in no uncertain terms that he had no idea of how long it would take to do any of the scheduled tasks. My frustration made me decide to hire a few key technical people to hopefully do what I could not get done by Ben and Mike.

It so happened that my need for qualified professional staff coincided with the liquidation of my old team from Spar's GSD, as Comstream unraveled. There were at least a dozen of top notch managers and engineers from GSD left without a job and I wasted no time in contacting them and offering them appropriate positions at NSI. Six months later I turned NSI into my former GSD, retaining only Ben, Mike, David, Mark and five other original NSI employees. Fifteen former Spar employees, all experts in satellite communication and VSAT technologies, joined me – their former boss - with enthusiasm and a will to succeed. It was a complete makeover for NSI and enabled us to bid on a major network extension in China, using C-band technologies that for years provided the bread and butter at GSD. A few months later, after the addition of a few more technical employees, we were better organized and more professional in everything we did, including budgeting, scheduling and producing technical documentation.

As a result, and under pressure from Steve and David, I decided to let Ben go, for he proved disruptive and inconclusive in his role as head of technology. In his place I appointed Claude H, a French man who occupied a similar position at Spar. Claude tried to organize and control Mike, but with no success. Mike's software development had become the major stumbling block and needed to be brought under control.

Mike was obviously using the lack of documentation as a bargaining chip, knowing that without him the VSAT development would have to be scrapped. We used both carrot and stick and told him in no uncertain terms that he had a choice to make – either cooperate and receive a big bonus on completing the development and properly documenting it, or be fired for insubordination. He eventually mellowed and agreed to have someone work side by side with him to document all his software work, claiming that he did not have the time to do both documentation and development.

By October 1996, almost a year after I took over, we managed to win a major contract from China for the extension of a C-band network initially built by Spar, using the same team now at NSI. The project was worth over $10 million and provided both the needed oxygen and a sense of renewed confidence in the future of the company. Our proprietary VSAT development, however, kept on stumbling from problem to problem.

In January 1997, I was asked to sign a $5,000 cheque for Steve Saviak. I was puzzled and asked David what that was all about. He told me that there was a verbal agreement with Steve to pay him $5000/month as consulting fees. I thought I was hearing things and asked for more information. He explained that during hard times Steve agreed to help out but wanted to be paid $5000/month for his work. I said I would not sign anything that is not duly formalized on paper. I told him I wanted to see a consulting contract spelling out his duties and accountabilities. I wanted to see a report on what he had done to deserve $5000/month. David was clearly unhappy at my request and informed Steve accordingly.

The following morning both Steve and his partner, also on the Board, came to see me wanting to know why I had a problem with the payment. I repeated that where I came from all payments are made against an invoice following a work order. I said I did not have a problem with giving Steve a consulting assignment, but I needed to make sure that whatever he was doing was in line with NSI needs and had to be formalized with a proper contract and a monthly report to me on services rendered. They were clearly taken aback, as they considered themselves my de-facto employers and did not appreciate my demands. Eventually, I did sign the cheque but I insisted on a formal contract for any further payments.

That incident marked the beginning of the end for my honeymoon with the controlling group of Board members, including David. From that point on I started to observe David more closely and discovered that he was frequently meeting with Steve behind closed doors. As part of my employment package I was due up to 50% yearly bonus based on performance. I did not expect that much, given our financial state, but I did expect a bonus based on what I did for the company in a very short time.

During my first Board meeting as CEO, it was decided that Steve would be in charge of writing a yearly performance report on my work so the Board could decide whether or not I deserved the bonus. When he kept delaying his report I suspected foul play and by mid-February I confronted him in private.

I asked him what his problem was and why he was not writing the report. He kept telling me that he was too busy but that he would as soon as he had the time. I reminded him that he had delayed the report for a full two months already and that I needed an explanation. I also told him that he was spending a lot of time with David behind closed doors and that I did not appreciate it. If he was doing important work on behalf of NSI I wanted to know what exactly he was up to. He mumbled a few excuses and promised to write my performance report by the end of that week. I did suspect foul play at that junction but I was not sure.

In his performance report on me, Steve was partly complimentary and partly critical, citing my inability to get the development of our proprietary VSAT completed. That report was the confirmation that he and David were plotting against me and I knew that my days were counted, for they had majority vote at Board meetings and could pass any resolution they wished against me.

At that point in time NSI had a solid organization, with clear management rules and a disciplined team of managers and technical experts to keep the company going. I was therefore less important to the company, but I did not worry at all. I continued to lead the company in my usual way, having become somewhat cavalier about the consequences. I did not dwell on the possibility that as CEO I could be overruled by my own CFO and a prima-donna member of the Board.

By June 1997 it became evident that our proprietary VSAT was not going anywhere, as Mike failed to make much progress and the system was irretrievably behind any acceptable schedule. In the meantime Spar was in great financial difficulties and was selling off whatever remaining assets they had. I took advantage of that situation and opened a dialogue with Spar for acquiring design rights and manufacturing tools associated with their Comstream VSAT product line. At the time I had a team of engineers and managers perfectly familiar with that technology and therefore capable of adopting it without any training. The acquisition would make it possible to liquidate NSI existing VSAT design effort, still plagued with unsolvable problems, and refocus the company on a working VSAT technology.

This new initiative is what Steve and David were actually waiting for to make their move. NSI had reached a point where it was essentially debt-free, well managed with formal accounting and planning techniques, and a team of professionals ready for any challenge. I had changed the DNA of the company and had put it on the map with the stock trading higher than ever following our contract in China. I had created the conditions and opened the door to the possibility of acquiring at a bargain price a working VSAT product line to satisfy our market needs. I also had established NSI as a credible satcom company with a solid reputation in traditional C-band networks, as proven by the Chinese contract.

NSI was therefore on temporarily solid financial grounds, but its future was not necessarily assured. With the impending acquisition of Comstream's technology and its installed base there were going to be challenges in managing successfully the migration of both technology and production activities from St Diego to Montreal. Without me at the helm, there was no one in the company with the necessary overall experience to manage the transition. But then again, I could have been wrong.

In August 1997, nearly two years after taking over as CEO, Steve and David asked me to resign. I knew it was coming and there was nothing I could do about it. They had the votes needed to oust me, just like they did with Ben two years earlier. They were good at that game and had no compunction about it. I could never agree to cook the books or do anything illegal, especially in a public company traded on the stock market. I had a fiduciary responsibility to all shareholders and was not about to compromise on my ethical conduct.

In a strange way this situation was a repeat of my predicament at Sovcanstar, both of which hinged on corporate honesty and fiduciary obligation to all shareholders. Steve and David were used to finagling in devious and questionable activities with small and start-up companies. I was not, and had no desire to learn. I therefore accepted a golden handshake and resigned. I felt hurt, wounded and for a while I isolated myself, meditating and trying to understand who I really was and why I seemed to get into similar situations. I could not trade personal integrity for personal gains. I could not do it. It was not in my DNA, period.

I left NSI at the age of 56, wondering whether I would be able to get back in the fray again. At that age and with my background at the top of the totem pole in large, medium and small companies, I knew I would find it difficult to re-enter the job market. No one would want to hire anyone who had been at higher management places, simply because they would worry about their own job. That's a fact of life. Managers at all levels feel secure only when there is no staff member smart enough to threaten their position. As a result, I could only hope to find a new job as the President of a small company, or as a VP of a medium-size public company, but those jobs where not plentiful, and the fact that I was forced to resign twice from my last two jobs did not help.

As well, we were entering an era of sustained high-tech business downturn, as the so-called 'bubble' burst right in the middle of my job search. By late 1998, many high-tech companies faced bankruptcy as the stock market tumbled following disappointing financial results. NSI too was forced into bankruptcy less than two years after I left, proving once again what bad management and personal greed can do.

Despite the bleak job market situation, I did manage to be appointed President and CEO of Incubanks Inc., an incubator company based in Los Angeles. The 'incubation' idea took hold in the hay-days of high-tech growth and gave birth to a few companies specializing in giving office space, management and financial support to young entrepreneurs with bright ideas. The funds were obtained from Venture Capitalists who provided seed money to anyone with the perceived ability to build a product (usually software based) and market it successfully. The new companies so created would then be taken to a stage where an IPO was justified, at which point the VCs would retreat with their pockets full of profit.

Incubanks was one of those companies, but it was late coming and never had a chance as the technology bubble burst while it was still in the making, and VC money was no longer available anywhere. I took over the company when it was essentially on its death bed and could do nothing to revive it.

Three months later, in January 2000, ended forever my management career. A couple of years thereafter, after turning sixty, I gave up trying.

***

Conclusion

It's always easy to judge, *a posteriori*, what was right and what was wrong in the way we conducted ourselves in our business career. It's easy to spot the good decisions and the bad decisions we made along the way. If we were to do it all over again, we would certainly change a number of bad decisions. But what really counts in the end is the overall result - not as a particular point in time, not in terms of how we live our retirement - but as a continuum of activities we lived through and opportunities we created for our family.

There will always be ups and downs in life, but as we add up all the plusses and minuses, we should be satisfied if we end up in positive territory, despite whatever reversal of fortunes we may experience at the end of it all. I would rather live a long life of riches that ends up in poverty than a long life of poverty tat ends up in riches.

I can therefore conclude that after living through a series of successes for most of my adult life, I cannot complain if in my final stretch as a retired old man I hit a reversal of fortunes. One might argue that, ideally, an exciting active life should be followed by an exciting retirement, but it doesn't always work that way.

I often think back and regurgitate the past, especially at night as I lay awake in bed trying in vain to fall asleep. I think of what it has been and what it could have been. I remember the honest mistakes and the wrong judgement calls, as I remember the brilliance of some of the decisions I made, too many to remember them all. For some reason though, it's mostly the mistakes that come back to haunt me. Would I make the same decisions if I could turn back the clock and relive the same situations? In most cases the answer is yes, I would repeat them all over again in all cases where honesty and fair play are at stake. That thought gives me peace of mind and puts a smile on my face because I know I have upheld my dignity and have been true to my principles as a man of integrity.

***

THE END

www.ingramcontent.com/pod-product-compliance
Lightning Source LLC
Chambersburg PA
CBHW070316190526
45169CB00005B/1653